BATTLEFIELD BRI

THE CIVIL WAR IN YORKSHIRE

FAIRFAX VERSUS NEWCASTLE

BATTLEFIELD BRITAIN

THE CIVIL WAR IN YORKSHIRE

FAIRFAX VERSUS NEWCASTLE

DAVID COOKE

Pen & Sword
MILITARY

To Jen

First published in Great Britain in 2004 by
PEN & SWORD MILITARY
an imprint of
Pen & Sword Books Limited
47 Church Street
Barnsley
South Yorkshire
S70 2AS

ISBN: 1 84415 076 3

A CIP catalogue record for this book
is available from the British Library

Typeset in 9pt Palatino by Pen & Sword Books Limited

Printed and bound in England by
CPI UK

Pen & Sword Books Ltd incorporates the imprints of
Pen & Sword Aviation, Pen & Sword Maritime, Pen & Sword Military,
Wharncliffe Local History, Pen & Sword Select,
Pen & Sword Military Classics and Leo Cooper

For a complete list of Pen & Sword titles please contact:
PEN & SWORD BOOKS LIMITED
47 Church Street, Barnsley, South Yorkshire, S70 2AS, England
email: enquiries@pen-and-sword.co.uk • website: www.pen-and-sword.co.uk

Contents

Preface 6

Chapter I   Horse, Foot and Guns
             – organisation and tactics of English Civil War armies 7
Chapter II   Opening Moves 14
Chapter III Fairfax stands his ground
             – the Battle of Tadcaster 21
Chapter IV   'The Rider of the White Horse'
             – the attack on Bradford and the storming of Leeds 29
Chapter V   'The greatest loss we ever received'
             – the Battle of Seacroft Moor 45
Chapter VI   'A Miraculous Victory'
             – the storming of Wakefield 53
Chapter VII 'A wild and desperate man'
             – the Battle of Adwalton Moor 61
Chapter VIII 'Pity poor Bradford'
             – the aftermath of Adwalton Moor and the fight
             at Selby 79
Chapter IX   Parliament resurgent
             – the storming of Selby 93
Chapter X   The great and close siege of York
             – the attack on the King's Manor 107
Chapter XI   'God made them stubble to our swords'
             – the Battle of Marston Moor 121
Chapter XII The fall of York and the end of the campaign in Yorkshire 145

Battlefield walks
Introduction
Walk One   The Battle of Tadcaster 160
Walk Two   The Storming of Leeds... 164
Walk Three   The Storming of Wakefield 168
Walk Four   The Battle of Adwalton Moor 170
Walk Five   The Actions at Selby.. 176
Walk Six   The Assault on the King's Manor............................... 180
Walk Seven   The Battle of Marston Moor 185

Bibliography and further reading 190
Index 191

Preface

The English Civil Wars took place throughout the country. Every county, town and village was affected, unlike any previous war in our nation's history. In the past, armies had marched and fought, and rulers had changed, but unless you were in the direct path of one of these armies war had little effect on your daily grind. The Civil Wars were different, particularly the 1st Civil War. Many towns, castles and houses were garrisoned, and these garrisons attempted to control the local area and levy taxes and supplies. When enemy garrisons were close to one another some unfortunates were taxed by both sides. Inevitably, the activities of these garrisons led to many small clashes, and when the larger field armies became involved these could escalate into major battles.

Yorkshire was no exception to this general pattern. Between December 1642 and July 1644, the Royalists and Parliamentarians vied for control of this vital recruiting ground and source of supplies. In the main the campaign was fought between the Earl of Newcastle's Royalist and Lord Fairfax's Parliamentary armies, although three other armies also converged on York for the climax of the campaign, the Battle of Marston Moor, the biggest and bloodiest battle of the Civil Wars and possibly the largest ever to have taken place on British soil. Another Yorkshire battle, at Adwalton Moor, caused such a fright in Parliament that an agreement was signed with Scotland, at that time a sovereign nation, which led to a large Scots army invading England in January 1644, an event that changed the whole course of the war.

The military actions in Yorkshire covered the whole gamut of seventeenth century warfare. The actions examined in this book include the defence of a town, two successful assaults on towns, a desperate rearguard action, the attempted storming of a breach during the largest siege of the Civil Wars, and a cavalry action on the streets of a town. The two largest actions include a true encounter battle, where two armies, each unaware of the other's presence, blundered into each other; and a full-blown set-piece battle, where both sides had the opportunity to deploy before battle was joined.

One of the main reasons for my interest in the Civil Wars is their immediacy, and one doesn't have to venture far to reach a site of interest. As a young boy I remember seeing the burnt-out ruins of a building in the centre of the village I was brought up in, Great Houghton, referred to by my father as the Old Hall. Many years later I discovered that this was the site of a small Civil War action in 1642, when a party of Colonel Washington's Royalist dragoons raided the hall during their march from the north-east to join the King's field army, although this was not when the hall was burnt down. It had survived as a public house well into the twentieth century. Where I now work, close to Barnsley, is within a few hundred yards of a battlefield at Tankersley. Several of the actions covered in this book took place within what are now town and city centres. Standing on Briggate in Leeds, looking down the hill, or outside Wakefield bus station, looking towards the town centre, you are at the centre of a Civil War battlefield.

CHAPTER I

Horse, Foot and Guns

– organisation and tactics of English Civil War armies

Before looking at the actions that took place within Yorkshire during the 1st Civil War, it is worth pausing to consider how the armies were recruited and organised, how they were equipped, and how they fought on the battlefield. It is also worth looking at how manpower and terrain affected the tactics employed by the commanders.

Recruitment

At the start of the Civil Wars most recruitment was on a voluntary basis, with both sides vying for control of the local trained bands, which were local militia forces that had experience of drill and weapons handling. Their armouries were a rich source of arms and armour, and both sides tried to gain control of these supplies.

In the lead up to the 1st Civil War, Parliament had raised an army to deal with the Catholic risings in Ireland, but few of these troops ever actually crossed the Irish Sea to fight, remaining in England and forming the basis of Parliament's main army, commanded by the Earl of Essex. On the Royalist side, the King issued commissions of array to many of his supporters, to raise regiments of foot, troops of horse, or both, usually at their own expense. Some of the King's more powerful supporters were given independent commands, and could issue their own commissions to allow others to raise regiments to serve under them. The Earl of Newcastle is a good example: he was given command of the northern counties, although Yorkshire was not part of his original remit, and he gathered a substantial force by commissioning certain officers to raise regiments.

Most units were raised by an individual officer, quite often a local magnate, who raised his regiment, or troop, from among his tenants. Others were professional soldiers who sent recruiting parties to local towns and villages to beat the drum. Some units came together in the initial flush of zeal, as in many other wars, and prominent members of local communities were given positions of authority, as with the London Trained Bands, many of which were formed by apprentices commanded by their masters.

As in any war, once the initial excitement had abated, the flow of volunteers began to dry up, and the armies had to employ other measures to bring in recruits. Both sides resorted to conscription within the areas they controlled, and if a town or village happened to be in a disputed area, it could be targeted by recruiting parties from both sides. These recruiting parties often used similar tactics to the Royal Navy press gangs of later years, riding into a village and leaving with as many able-bodied men as they could find.

Another source of recruits was enemy prisoners. Early in the wars, regular prisoner exchanges took place, but the value of prisoners as additional manpower was soon realised. The lot of a low-ranking prisoner was not a happy one, and many, with no strongly held political or religious beliefs, volunteered to fight for their captors. At other times prisoners were forced to join the enemy ranks, as with the defenders of Rotherham in early May 1643. When the Earl of Newcastle took the town its defenders were forced to join his army. A Royalist source states that they volunteered, while a Parliamentary source states quite clearly that they were pressed into service. Rotherham was a staunchly Protestant town, so the latter account is more likely.

A sometimes overlooked source of manpower was the local volunteer force, often referred to in Yorkshire as 'clubmen'. These units would be raised on an ad hoc basis. In the campaign in Yorkshire they were used mainly by the Fairfaxes, who supplemented their regular troops with large numbers of local volunteers at encounters including Leeds, Seacroft Moor and Adwalton Moor. A setback to a force containing a contingent of clubmen could have a major effect on the economy of the home town of the recruits, as was shown after the capture of a large number of men from Bradford and Halifax at Seacroft Moor.

However the armies were recruited, manpower was always a problem. Rather than keeping existing regiments up to strength, commissions were issued to raise new units, and with only a finite number of men available, many units sank to ridiculously low strengths.

Organisation and equipment

A regiment of foot had a theoretical establishment of 1,200 men. These were divided into ten companies: colonel, lieutenant-colonel, major, and seven captains. The higher the rank, the larger the company, so while the colonel's company had almost 200 men, each captain's company had only 100.

It was very difficult to keep a regiment at full strength, or even to recruit it to anywhere near 1,200 men. Disease, detachments and battlefield casualties rapidly reduced the strength of a regiment, and there are numerous records of regiments less than 200 men strong. While some regiments actually exceeded their paper strength, and there are even records of double strength regiments, most were well below this, and it was quite common on the battlefield to combine several regiments into a single tactical unit. With the exception of Newcastle's own regiment, this was certainly the case with the remainder of Newcastle's Northern

Foot, and with Lord Fairfax's infantry at the Battle of Marston Moor.

Another problem throughout the Civil Wars was that while regiments fielded a fraction of their paper strength, most had a full complement of officers, with, on occasion, a company of fifteen to twenty men having three officers. When Parliament formed the New Model Army in early 1645, hundreds of officers had to resign their commissions, or continue to serve as volunteers. Unfortunately, the Royalist armies never went through such a remodelling and many, if not most, Royalist regiments were massively over-officered throughout the Civil Wars.

Each company was divided into two parts, pike and musket. The ideal ratio was one pike for each two muskets, but early in the Civil Wars this was not always achieved, particularly by the Royalists, with ratios of 1:1 and 2:3 being found in some units. Later in the wars, when manpower became a problem, particularly for the Royalists, the number of pikes in a unit was reduced as musketeers were deemed to be more useful. Some Royalist infantry units at Naseby in June 1645 went to the extreme of having no pikes at all. Manpower was a problem for the Fairfaxes from the start of the wars, and on a number of occasions, including Seacroft Moor and Adwalton Moor, they had no pikemen with them at all.

The company was more of an administrative unit than a tactical one. When the regiment was deployed for battle, the pike contingent from each company was massed in the centre of the unit, with the regiment's musketeers divided in two and positioned to each side of the pike block. When the tactical situation warranted, the pike and shot could be separated and fight independently. An example of this was at Adwalton Moor, where the Royalist army's musketeers were sent forward to occupy an area of enclosures, while the pikemen remained on the open moor to their rear.

In theory a pikeman should have been well armoured, with a breast and back plate to protect his body, a gorget to cover his throat, tassets to protect his thighs, and a pot (helmet) on his head. This was a large amount of metal to be carrying on a hot day. Fortunately for the poor pikeman, very few were equipped to this level, and the ones that were quickly discarded all but their helmets. For weapons the pikeman carried a pike, as his name suggests, and a sword. The pike was supposed to be sixteen feet long, but, for ease of use, was quite often cut down to around twelve feet, the other four feet providing a good source of firewood! The sword was of very poor quality, having been mass-produced by the thousand, and would have been more use for chopping wood than killing an opponent.

The musketeer provided the regiment with its firepower, and was equipped with a matchlock musket. This got its name from the match, a slow-burning cord that was used to discharge the weapon. He was also equipped with a similar sword to the pikeman, but more often preferred to use the butt end of his musket as a close-quarter weapon, and a very effective one it proved to be. Musketeers were very versatile troops. As well as supporting the regiment, they could also be detached as 'commanded' musketeers, operating independently or supporting the regiments of horse on an army's flanks.

The horse on both sides were equipped in a similar manner, and are referred to in contemporary military manuals as 'arquebusiers', although the term was rarely used in contemporary accounts, which usually refer to the mounted troops as horse. The standard equipment for a trooper was a sturdy long-sleeved buff leather coat, with a breast and back plate to cover his vitals. On his legs he wore a pair of thick thigh-length boots, and his head was covered by a helmet, often referred to as a lobster pot because of its articulated neck guard, which resembled a lobster's tail. For weapons he carried a good-quality sword, a pair of pistols and a carbine. This was the ideal equipment for a trooper, but many of them were nowhere near as well equipped as this, and some could be found on the field wearing their normal daily clothes, armed only with a sword.

Unlike an infantry company, which was a purely administrative unit, the troop, the mounted equivalent, was also a tactical unit. The establishment of a troop was set at 60 men, although numbers varied considerably. Troops could operate independently, but were usually combined into regiments, and, once again, the number of troops within a regiment could vary considerably.

Dragoons were jacks of all trades. Equipped in a similar fashion to the musketeers, they rode to battle, usually dismounting to fight. They were organised into companies, and a number of companies made up a regiment, although dragoon companies often operated independently. It was not unknown for a few dragoons to be included within a troop of horse, to provide the troop with additional firepower. Dragoons had many uses, from reconnaissance to supporting the horse on the battlefield.

The final part of a Civil War army was the artillery, which included light mobile field guns and heavy siege weapons, which were almost immobile on the battlefield. Artillery seems to have had very little effect on the battlefield, and is quite often mentioned in contemporary accounts as an afterthought in a list of captured material, if it is mentioned at all.

Tactics

Before looking at the tactic used by both sides, it is worth considering the military experience of the officers and commanders during the Civil Wars. Many of the officers, of all ranks, had little if any military experience, and relied on the knowledge of experienced professional officers, who had learnt their trade on the Continent.

Neither of the senior commanders in the campaign for Yorkshire had much military background. Lord Ferdinando Fairfax had been sent to the Continent as a young man by his father, who wanted him to be a soldier, but seems to have been a failure as a soldier. During the 1st Bishops' War he commanded a regiment of Yorkshire Trained Bands foot, but he took no active part in the 2nd Bishops' War. Similarly, William Cavendish, Earl of Newcastle, had commanded troops during the Bishops' Wars, having raised a troop of horse at his own expense, although his major contribution was monetary, having donated a massive £10,000 to the King's cause.

Both commanders owed their positions to their standing within the community. Both also seem to have relied on more experienced advisors. In the case of Lord

Ferdinando, Lord Fairfax (1584-1648)

Ferdinando, Lord Fairfax, was born in 1584, son of Thomas Fairfax, 1st Baron. His father wanted him to be a soldier, and is reported to have said 'I sent him to the Netherlands to train him up a soldier and he makes a tolerable country justice, but is a mere coward at fighting'. His father became 1st Baron Fairfax in 1627, a title to which Ferdinando succeeded on 1 May 1640.

During the latter part of the reign of James I, and the early part of that of Charles I, Fairfax served in Parliament as the member for Boroughbridge. In the 1st Bishops' War he commanded a regiment of the Yorkshire Trained Bands, but does not seem to have taken an active part in the 2nd Bishops' War. During the Long Parliament he represented the county of York,

and was one of the representatives sent to present the Grand Remonstrance to the King. When the King moved from London to York in the lead up to the 1st Civil War, Fairfax was a member of the five-man committee despatched by Parliament to represent it, and to keep a close eye on the King's actions.

In early September 1642 he was chosen to lead Parliament's supporters within Yorkshire, a choice ratified by Parliament on 27 September. A treaty of neutrality was signed by both parties, but Fairfax said it must be agreed to by Parliament, which then annulled the treaty.

Fairfax, after establishing his base among the mill towns of the West Riding, began to make headway against the Royalists, until the arrival of the Earl of Newcastle's army in December 1642. The campaign of 1643 culminated in his defeat at Adwalton Moor, and although Fairfax does not seem to have been a natural soldier, he was determined enough to continue the fight. In 1644 his fortunes turned, with the Scots invasion of northern England, and the victory of the Allied army at Marston Moor, where he was one of the commanders, changed the face of the war in Yorkshire, and throughout the nation, although his son Charles was killed during the battle.

After Marston Moor Fairfax continued to command the Yorkshire forces, while his son, Sir Thomas, went on to command the New Model Army. Fairfax slowly, but surely, continued to reduce the Royalist garrisons in the county, until, on 21 December 1645, the final garrison, Skipton Castle, capitulated.

On 14 March 1648 he died of injuries he had sustained in an accident. Fairfax was not a natural commander, but had sufficient determination to carry the war in Yorkshire through to its conclusion. He was well respected by his enemies, and part of York's articles of surrender was that Fairfax, and his men, formed York's garrison. Many towns were pillaged once they had surrendered, but this did not happen at York, and the grateful citizens raised a plaque to Lord Fairfax in the Chapter House of York Minster, where it remains to this day.

Fairfax he seems to have depended very much on his son, Sir Thomas, who had gained some experience of his own on the Continent and in the Bishops' Wars, and who would eventually rise to the highest military command in the country. Newcastle, on the other hand, had an experienced Scots professional soldier at his disposal – James King. King had fought on the Continent during the Thirty Years War. While Sir Thomas Fairfax was young and willing to take chances, and learn from his mistakes, King was very cautious, and it is possible that Newcastle missed several strategic opportunities because of King's more measured approach.

Many regimental commanders also suffered from a lack of military experience, and experienced field officers were actively sought to serve under them, quite often taking command of the regiment in the field while the colonel remained in a safe rear echelon post. A good example of this is in the Scots army that invaded England in January 1644. Most of the regimental colonels were members of the aristocracy, with little military knowledge, while most of the lieutenant-colonels and majors were more experienced, having served on the Continent, particularly in the Swedish service.

There were also gifted amateurs, who had no experience at all of soldiering, but who took to the military way of life quickly. A fine example is Oliver Cromwell, who raised a troop of horse at the start of the 1st Civil War, mainly because of his position as a local squire and Member of Parliament. He rose to the highest rank in the land, and proved to be one of the finest cavalry commanders in British history.

The military manuals of the time, and the wars on the Continent, gave rise to two different schools of thought about tactics that could be employed by the horse and foot, known as the Dutch and Swedish methods. Both had their supporters, and both were tried at the start of the Civil Wars in England. It is beyond the scope of this book to give a detailed description of these tactical approaches, but a brief explanation may be of use.

The regiments of foot would normally be formed into brigades of two to four regiments. In the Swedish system the pikemen of each regiment would form separately to the musketeers, with the four pike blocks within the brigade forming a diamond shape. Numerous small bodies of musketeers were deployed to the front, flanks and rear of the pike blocks. This was a complex system, and beyond the capabilities of the barely trained soldiers to perform, or their inexperienced officers to carry out.

The Dutch system was much more straightforward, and as many more Englishmen had served in the Dutch service, the system was more familiar. Once again, a number of regiments formed a brigade, but each regiment formed as an integral unit, with the pike in the centre and the muskets on each flank. The brigade would often be formed in two lines, with the regiments in the second line covering the gaps in the first. In general, the Dutch system was adopted by both sides, as well as the Scots.

With the horse, the difference between the two systems was not in how the units deployed, but in how they actually fought: shock action versus fire-power. The Swedish system had the horse charging at the gallop with the sword, and only resorting to pistols once the mêlée had commenced. The shock of the charge would often break the enemy very quickly. This system was adopted almost universally by the Royalists, while their opponents initially adopted the Dutch system, which relied on fire-power to stop the enemy charge, followed by a swift counter-charge. During the early part of the 1st Civil War most Parliamentary units adopted this strategy, which proved unsuccessful against the Royalist break-neck charge, as was shown at Powick Bridge and Edgehill. One exception to this was Lord Fairfax's horse, which adopted the Swedish system like their Royalist opponents.

One major drawback of the charge at the gallop was controlling the horsemen once the charge had been successful. On many occasions this led to the Royalist horse galloping from the field in pursuit of their defeated opponents, and three of the major battles of the Civil Wars saw examples of this. At Edgehill the Royalist horse was victorious on both flanks, but then left the field in a mad pursuit. While they were away the Royalist foot came close to being defeated, and a resounding Royalist victory was turned into a drawn fight. At Marston Moor and Naseby the lack of control of the Royalist horse, victorious on one flank, led directly to a Royalist defeat.

With the lack of success of their fire-power tactics, the Parliamentary horse evolved new strategies to counter the enemy's charge. They reverted to shock tactics, but charged at the trot, not at the gallop, enabling their commanders to keep more control. At Marston Moor and Naseby, while the Royalist horse won on one flank, the Parliamentary horse, commanded by Oliver Cromwell on both occasions, won on the other. Because they were still under control, they were able to turn onto the flank of the enemy centre and play a major part in their defeat. At both battles the Royalist infantry, after initial success, were defeated and incurred horrendous casualties.

On an open field, the standard deployment of a Civil War army was with the foot in the centre and the horse on both wings. The army, both horse and foot regiments, would be deployed in two lines. One major variant on this was if the foot of one side were heavily outnumbered, when a reserve of horse could be placed to support them, as was done by the Royalists at Marston Moor and Naseby. While the foot advanced to 'push of pike', the horse on either wing tried to defeat their opponents. If successful they would then turn into the enemy foot.

As will be seen, only one action covered in this book was fought on open ground in the form described above. Tadcaster, Bradford, Leeds, Wakefield and Selby were all attacks on fortified towns, and each followed a similar course. The foot of the attacking force would assault the barricades at one or more street end, trying to force a way into the street. Once the barricade was cleared, the waiting horse would charge into the town to disrupt the enemy. Seacroft Moor was a fighting retreat, where a raiding force was caught withdrawing and, unable to reach the safety of a large area of enclosures, was caught on the open moor and defeated by a large force of enemy cavalry. Adwalton Moor, although a field battle, was affected by the terrain, particularly the enclosures bordering the north-west side of the moor. It was only once the Parliamentary troops had begun to deploy onto the open moor that the bulk of the Royalist army could get at them, defeating them in the process.

Terrain, experience, forces available and a multitude of other factors affected how a commander fought in any action. As will be seen in the following chapters, this meant that no two English Civil War battles were the same.

CHAPTER II

Opening Moves

Thus my Lord marched into the town with great joy,
to the general satisfaction both of the nobility
and gentry, and most of the citizens. Duchess of Newcastle

The Civil War came early to Yorkshire. Although many people date the start of the conflict from 22 August 1642, when King Charles I raised his royal standard at Nottingham, forces had been gathering throughout the country, and skirmishes had been fought prior to this date. The raising of the standard marked the final break between the King and his Parliament.

Charles had ruled without recourse to Parliament for most of his reign. Some of the measures to which he had resorted to raise money during this period had caused an undercurrent of dissatisfaction. For example, many of his subjects from inland counties protested about having to pay Ship Money, a tax normally levied only on coastal counties. Some took the protest as far as refusing to pay and serving a term in jail. Another way the King raised money was through the sale of titles and positions, which was an unpopular measure.

In addition many people were also worried by the King's approach to religion. Followers of the Nonconformist sects, usually referred to as Puritans, were very concerned about reforms, and there was a steady flow of emigrants across the Atlantic to the New England colonies. To some the King's reforms seemed to be moving back towards Catholicism, and the fact that the Queen was a practising Catholic, and had great influence over the King, reinforced this idea. In reality Charles had no serious intention of allowing the Catholic faith to become England's, or Scotland's, state religion.

In 1639 Charles's attempts to impose his religious reforms on the Scots, including the introduction of bishops into the Church of Scotland, led to the first open breach between Charles and his subjects – the 1st Bishops' War. Charles was in desperate need of funds to fight the Scots, and decided to recall Parliament, which proved obstructive to his aims. The conflict was resolved without recourse to arms, and Charles returned to his autocratic rule by dissolving this unruly gathering, known to posterity as the Short Parliament. Charles does not seem to have learned from his mistakes, however. He continued to try to force his religious reforms on the Scots, and in 1640 war broke out again – the 2nd Bishops' War. This time matters did come to a military conclusion: the Scots advanced into England and defeated the English at Newburn, and in the aftermath of their victory occupied Newcastle. Charles had no option but to recall Parliament, and, with the deteriorating military situation, was in no position to dissolve it again. This Parliament would become known as the Long Parliament.

Charles's poor financial position made it difficult for him to resist Parliament's demands for changes in the way England was governed, and slowly the breach between King and Parliament grew. At the same time Parliament was split between those members who supported the King and those who opposed him. This opposition took two main forms, political and religious, and it is worth pausing to consider this. The Hothams, who figured prominently in the story of the first year of the Civil War in Yorkshire, had differing reasons for opposing the King. Sir John Hotham seems to have had both political and more personal reasons for his position: the King had appointed one of Hotham's rivals as Governor of Hull, a position Sir John coveted, and this seems to have pushed him into Parliament's fold. His son, Captain John Hotham, was of a puritanical persuasion, which seems to have been the main motive for him following his father's lead in supporting Parliament.

Because of the nature of the arguments for and against the King's policies, many families and friends were divided. The most famous example of this is of two friends, and Members of Parliament, Sir Ralph Hopton and Sir William Waller. Both had served together on the Continent as young men, and they had been friends for many years. Both believed that the King's policies were wrong, but Hopton could not bring himself to fight against his King, while Waller could. They became opponents in the fiercely fought campaign for the south-western counties, but continued to correspond with one another throughout. It is worth noting that many Parliamentary supporters insisted that they were not fighting against the King, but against his 'wicked advisors'.

Opposition to the King began to coalesce around five members of the House of Commons: John Pym, John Hampden, Denzil Holles, Sir Arthur Haselrigg and William Strode. On 4 January 1642 the King attempted to carry out a pre-emptive strike, by entering Parliament with an armed escort and arresting the five members. They had been warned of Charles's plan and had fled downriver into the heart of London. Seeing that they were not present, Charles said, 'The birds have flown'. There was widespread support for Parliament in the city, and Charles decided it would be prudent to leave. While the five members returned to Parliament in triumph, Charles left London for Windsor. The next time he entered the city he would be on trial for his life.

On 31 January Sir John Hotham arrived at Hull to assume the governorship of the town for Parliament, having vowed that he would hold the town 'fall back, fall edge'. Hull was an important port, and the major arms magazine in the north of England, and its possession would provide major advantages for its occupier in the coming conflict. As Parliament began to prepare for war, so too did the King. On 23 February the Queen sailed for Holland, with the objective of selling many of the crown jewels to raise money to buy arms and equipment for the King's fledgling army.

Once his wife had departed for the Continent the King began to move north, and by 19 March he had arrived at his northern capital, York. Things began to move more rapidly when, on 9 April, Parliament petitioned the King to move the magazine at Hull to the safety of the Tower of London. Although Hull's governor, Sir John Hotham, was a Parliamentary supporter, they still thought the King's proximity to Hull endangered their control of the arms and powder held there. The King also recognised the importance of possessing the town, as not only did it contain a major magazine, but it also provided an ideal point of return for the Queen, and the arms consignment she would be bringing with her in due course. With this in mind he attempted to gain possession of the town.

Initially he sent his son, the Duke of York, to visit the town on 22 April, and the prince was received with the utmost courtesy. On the following day the King himself arrived before the gates of Hull, where, in the first overt act of opposition, Sir John Hotham refused him entry. The King was attended by a large, armed entourage, which escorted him to Beverley when admission to Hull was denied. On 24 April Sir John Hotham was declared a traitor by a royal herald in front of the Beverley Gate, but even this dramatic turn of events did not prompt him to open the gates to the King's supporters.

On 14 May the King summoned all the horse of Yorkshire to attend him at York. When news of this reached Parliament, the sheriffs of the counties surrounding Yorkshire were ordered to prevent troops passing through their territory to join the King. On 3 June a meeting of the Yorkshire gentry was held at Heworth Moor, near York, during which a young Yorkshire gentleman attempted to hand a petition to the King, and was barged by the King's horse in the process. This young man was Sir Thomas Fairfax, and Sir Clement Markham, his biographer, writes that:

> Fairfax was not a man to be turned from his purpose by any such obstacles. He at last succeeded in forcing his way to the King's side, and in placing the petition on the pommel of his saddle. Charles was obliged to learn that many of the Yorkshire gentry strongly disapproved of his proceedings in raising troops.

Little did the King know that the young gentleman Fairfax would become one of the agents of his downfall.

Sir Thomas Fairfax (1612-1671)

Sir Thomas, the eldest son of Ferdinando, Lord Fairfax, was born at Denton in Yorkshire on 17 January 1612. Having gained some military experience in the Low Countries, he commanded a troop of dragoons during the 1st Bishops' War, for which he was knighted in January 1640.

During the early part of the 1st Civil War he acted as his father's second-in-command. He took part in a number of actions, with varying degrees of success, during 1643: Leeds (23 January), Seacroft Moor (30 April), Wakefield (21 May) and Adwalton Moor (30 June). Following a heavy defeat at Adwalton Moor, Lord Fairfax's army withdrew into Hull, where it remained until April 1644. In the interim Parliament had found further employment for Sir Thomas. Initially he crossed the Humber with his father's horse and joined with the Army of the Eastern Association during its campaign in Lincolnshire. He was then tasked with gathering forces for the relief of Nantwich, which he carried out successfully, beating the Royalists at Nantwich on 25 January 1644.

With the Scots invasion in January 1644, Fairfax returned to Yorkshire, joining with his father's forces to storm Selby on 11 April. There followed a gathering of forces, drawn towards York, which was besieged by Parliament and the Scots. The climax of the campaign came at the battle of Marston Moor (2 July). Although Fairfax's troops were driven from the field, he seems to have come out of the battle with his reputation enhanced, having ridden alone around the Royalist army to Cromwell's wing, being wounded in the process.

Sir Thomas was a brave and accomplished soldier, as his subsequent career shows. On 21 January 1645 he was appointed commander of the New Model Army, and led it to victory at Naseby (14 June). He continued to command throughout the 1st and 2nd Civil Wars, to victory in both cases. He protested against the King's trial and resigned his command in 1650. During the Commonwealth he remained in the background, but returned to royal favour after assisting in the Restoration of Charles II.

As the antagonism between the King and his Parliament increased, the King continued to recruit his forces, as did his opponents. If the dispute turned into open warfare, the troops raised at York would form the basis of his marching army. On 2 July the King was dealt another blow when the fleet declared its support for Parliament, making possession of Hull even more important. On the same day a Royalist warship, the *Providence*, was captured by the Parliamentarians, but managed to escape with its cargo of gunpowder, which proved to be a great boon to the Royalists.

Another small vessel had been captured at the same time as the *Providence*, but was successfully escorted into Hull. On board was a man masquerading as a

Frenchman, who turned out to be Lord George Digby, one of the King's chief supporters, and very high on Parliament's list of 'wicked advisors'. Lord George was acting as a messenger between the Queen, now in Holland, and the King at York, and was travelling in disguise. Digby declared his identity to Sir John Hotham, and the pair seem to have come to an agreement: if the King laid siege to Hull, Sir John would surrender the town to him. Digby carried this message to the King, and the fledgling Royalist army moved to Beverley on 8 July, and then on to Hull on 10 July. By coincidence Parliament had despatched 500 reinforcements to Hull, under the command of Sir John Meldrum, an experienced Scots soldier, and these arrived as the Royalists were laying down their siege lines outside the town. Medrum's arrival seems to have strengthened Hotham's resolve, and the town remained firmly in Parliamentary hands. Leaving the siege in the less than capable hands of the Earl of Newport, the King began to move south, lodging at Doncaster on 20 July and reaching Nottingham on 21 July. Towards the end of the month Meldrum launched a sortie from Hull, which drove the Royalist besiegers back to Beverley and broke the siege.

With the departure of the King and a major part of the forces he had raised in Yorkshire, the situation in the county was confused, with both sides trying to raise forces and gain a position of advantage over their opponents. The Earl of Cumberland, a senior Yorkshire nobleman, but no soldier, commanded the main Royalist force, which was based at York. He was opposed by three Parliamentary forces. In the West Riding mill towns, particularly Bradford and Halifax, Lord Fairfax and his son began to raise a small force, while in Hull the Hothams, father and son, had the town's garrison at their disposal. Finally, Sir Hugh Cholmley commanded the garrison of Scarborough, another major east coast port, which, with Hull, gave Parliament control of most of Yorkshire's coast. This was a grave disadvantage to the Royalist war effort as the Queen would need to land somewhere on the north-east coast during the spring, with her vital cargo of arms and ammunition.

A period of relative quiet followed the King's departure, and a nervous neutrality seems to have existed between the two sides. Towards the end of the year things began to warm up again, with a series of raids and counter-raids, during which the Parliamentary forces seem to have gained the upper hand. Cumberland, who admitted that he was no soldier, was finding it difficult to keep the Parliamentarians at bay. On 26 September a number of important Yorkshire gentry wrote a letter to the Earl of Newcastle asking for his assistance. Newcastle had been given a commission to command in the four northern counties, Durham, Northumberland, Cumberland and Westmoreland, where he was busy raising and equipping a substantial force. On 30 September Newcastle replied with a number of propositions. First, that his army should be paid while they were in Yorkshire, and that an assessment should be made on the county to provide the money, and if no such payment was forthcoming his soldiers would be provided with free billets. His officers would also receive pay from the same assessment. Second, that his troops would be provided with provisions as soon as they entered the county. Thirdly, since one of the missions he had been given was to protect the Queen when she arrived, Newcastle would not be in breach of his agreement if he withdrew his army to carry out what he saw as his main task.

William Cavendish, Duke of Newcastle (1592-1676)

William Cavendish was born in 1592 and educated at St John's College, Cambridge. In 1610, as part of the celebrations following the investiture of Prince Henry, Charles's older brother, as the Prince of Wales, he was made a Knight of the Bath. Following a tour of the Continent, he returned to England and married Elizabeth, daughter of William Basset of Blore in Staffordshire. Further promotions in the peerage followed, first to Viscount Mansfield on 3 November 1620, and then to Earl of Newcastle on 7 March 1628.

Newcastle was one of the richest men in the country, as was illustrated by the amount of money he paid to entertain the King during two visits, one to Welbeck and the other to Bolsover: £20,000. Newcastle's ambitions were satisfied when he was appointed Lord-Lieutenant of Derbyshire (1628-38) and Wiltshire (1626-42). He was also appointed governor to the Prince of Wales in 1638, and promoted to the King's privy council.

During the Bishops' Wars Newcastle donated £10,000 to the King's coffers, and raised a volunteer troop of horse from knights and gentlemen of quality. During this period he clashed with the Earl of Holland and almost fought a duel with him. The hostility of the earls of Holland and Essex caused him to retire from court and resign his position as the Prince's governor. In January 1642 he was at Hull, attempting, unsuccessfully, to seize the town for the King.

Newcastle was appointed commander of the northern counties, and began to raise an army in Northumberland and County Durham. In December 1642, at the behest of the Yorkshire Royalists, he moved his army into Yorkshire, where he fought a series of actions against Lord Fairfax's Parliamentary army. The high point of this campaign was his victory over Fairfax at Adwalton Moor in June 1643, which led to Parliament signing an agreement with the Scots, and Newcastle's elevation to the rank of Marquess. January 1644 saw the Scots invade northern England, and although Newcastle put up a valiant defence, the Royalist defeat at Marston Moor saw his army destroyed.

With his fortune gone, and his army destroyed, Newcastle decided to leave for the Continent, rather than face the mockery of some members of the court. He remained in exile until the Restoration of Charles II in 1660, when he returned to England and was promoted to Duke of Newcastle for his services to the King's father. During his exile he met and married Margaret Lucas, sister of Sir Charles Lucas.

Newcastle had no real military experience when he took over command of the Royalist army in the north, and received the commission because of his rank and the fact that he had money to raise an army. He relied on experienced military advisors, James King in particular. King was a slow but steady commander, which can be seen in the campaign of 1643, and may have had some responsibility for Newcastle's army not marching south after Adwalton Moor. Newcastle was also an excellent horseman, and wrote several treatises on horsemanship.

Musketeers and guns open fire. Courtesy of John Wilson

Newcastle received a positive response to his propositions, with the Yorkshire gentlemen agreeing to everything except the pay for his officers. Once this was settled Newcastle planned to move south, but this was not until he had finished training and equipping his army in late November. Using his time well, Newcastle fortified and garrisoned a number of towns in the north east. By 1 December his army was marching into Yorkshire, when a small Parliamentary force tried to stop him at Piercebridge, where the road crossed the Tees. The Parliamentarians were quickly put to flight and Newcastle's advance continued. In the meantime Lord Fairfax had gathered a sizeable force together and began to move towards York, but the news of the defeat at Piercebridge brought him to a halt at Tadcaster. His son, Sir Thomas Fairfax, had occupied quarters at Wetherby, where he was attacked by a raiding force despatched from York by the city's governor, Sir Thomas Glemham, but after a short, sharp fight the Royalists were driven off.

On 3 December Newcastle's army arrived at York, and the Duchess of Newcastle, his wife, describes his reception:

> Being come to York he [Newcastle] drew up his army before the time [agreed], both horse and foot, where the Commander-in-Chief, the then Earl of Cumberland, together with the gentry of the country, came to wait on my Lord, and the then Governor of York, Sir Thomas Glemham, presented him with the keys of the city.
>
> Thus my Lord marched into the town with great joy, and to the general satisfaction both of the nobility and gentry, and most of the citizens.

With Newcastle's arrival the situation in Yorkshire had completely changed, with 6,000 well-armed troops having arrived to supplement the Yorkshire Royalist forces, and now Lord Fairfax and Captain John Hotham found themselves heavily outnumbered. The stage was set for the opening of the main campaign to control Yorkshire, which was a vital recruiting ground and supply source for the Royalist war effort. It also provided a road south for the north-eastern counties, which were rich recruiting grounds. Much of the King's marching army had been raised in Yorkshire, Durham and Northumberland, and had marched off to the south with him in July. Whoever had control of York had control of the county, and the road south. Later in the war King Charles wrote a letter to his nephew, Prince Rupert, stressing the importance of relieving York, which was besieged by the Scots and Parliament. In it he stated that 'If York be lost I shall esteem my crown little else'.

CHAPTER III

Fairfax stands his ground
– the Battle of Tadcaster

But the enemy pressing still on us,
forced us to draw back and maintain that ground. Sir Thomas Fairfax

With the arrival at York, and his assumption of command of the Yorkshire Royalist forces, the Earl of Newcastle decided to act quickly and attack Lord Fairfax's army at Tadcaster. In the hope of trapping and destroying the Parliamentary force Newcastle decided on a two-pronged attack, with the bulk of his army – the foot, artillery, and a number of troops of horse – attacking Tadcaster from the east, while the Earl of Newport, his Lieutenant-General, with the remainder of the horse, would carry out a night march via Wetherby and attack Tadcaster from the west. During 6 December the Royalist forces began to move, Newcastle's contingent quartering in the villages to the east of Tadcaster, while Newport began his night march towards Wetherby.

Lord Fairfax had gathered all his available forces together at Tadcaster on hearing of Newcastle's approach to York, calling Captain John Hotham's force back from its quarters in Wetherby. A council of war was called to decide on a course of action. Sir Thomas Fairfax writes that 'the Town was judged untenable, and that we should draw out to an advantageous piece of ground by the town'. It is difficult to gauge where this piece of ground was. It is obvious, with Newcastle approaching from the east, and the subsequent course of the battle, that the ground lay on the west side of the River Wharfe, one possibility being the enclosed ground between Tadcaster and Bramham Moor, a piece of ground Sir Thomas would use to delay a much larger enemy force in March 1643. Where the Parliamentary force intended to make its stand must remain a moot point, as the rapid Royalist advance on the morning of 7 December prevented this plan from being carried out.

With Newcastle's army rapidly approaching it is time to look at the ground upon which the battle would be fought. The Duchess of Newcastle gives a good description:

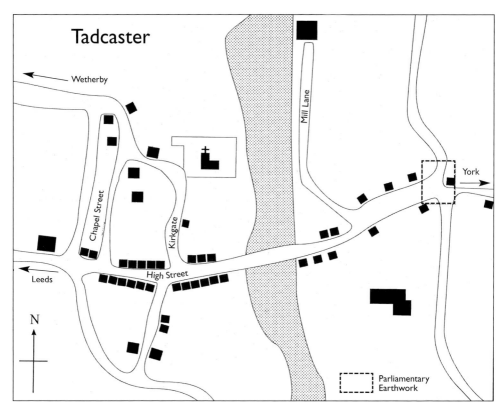

Looking east over the bridge at Tadcaster towards the Parliamentary earthwork and the road to York.

Musketeers firing a volley. Courtesy John Wilson

> The greatest part of the town stands on the west side of a river [the
> Wharfe] not fordable in any place near thereabout, nor allowing any
> passage into the town from York, but over a stone-bridge which the
> enemy had made impassable by breaking down part of the bridge and
> planting their ordnance upon it, and by raising a very large and strong
> fort upon the top of a hill, leading eastward from that bridge towards
> York, upon design of commanding the bridge and all other places fit to
> draw up an army in, or to plant cannon against them.

In 1642 the main part of Tadcaster lay on the west side of the Wharfe, as it still does.
Interestingly, the street plan as it existed at the time can still be traced today.
Running west from the bridge ran the High Street, both sides of which were lined
with houses, each having its own enclosed garden to the rear. A lane, Kirkgate, ran
north from the main street, about 50 yards west of the bridge, to St Mary's church.
A similar distance further west another lane, Chapel Street, ran north to join with
Kirkgate, and then turned west towards Wetherby. To the south of the main street
two other lanes ran south, to join together just beyond the southern end of the
town, continuing on towards Sherburn-in-Elmet. It is difficult to believe but this
was the Great North Road, the precursor of the modern A1.

On the east side of the bridge the road continues towards York, sweeping
slightly to the left as it ascends the hill, before gently turning towards the right as
it crosses the crest and begins to descend. It was at this point that Lord Fairfax had
raised an earthwork to protect the road to York and prevent the Royalists planting
their cannon on the ridge to bombard the town. The extent of this earthwork is

difficult to judge, with contemporary writers disagreeing about the extent of the fortification. Sir Henry Slingsby simply describes them as 'their works', giving no clue at all about their size, while Sir Thomas Fairfax writes of a 'slight work', and his father of 'some breast-works for our musketeers'. On the other hand the Duchess of Newcastle writes of a 'very large and strong fort upon the top of a hill'. It is interesting that two accounts, Sir Henry Slingsby and Lord Fairfax, speak of breastworks as opposed to a single earthwork. Although the area is now completely built over it can still be seen that there was no room for the 'very large and strong fort' described by the Duchess, as there is little level ground before the road begins to descend. There were several buildings close to the spot in 1611, so if they still existed in 1642 they, and their enclosures, could have been used as part of the Parliamentary defences. However large the earthwork was it would prove to be a major obstacle to the Royalist attack.

Just to the east of the bridge a lane, Mill Lane, ran north towards a mill on the banks of the Wharfe. A weir still marks the site of the mill flue. A number of buildings stood around the junction of the York road and Mill Lane, which would play a prominent part in the battle. The bridge itself had been prepared for defence by demolishing part of the roadway between two of the piers. To allow access back and forth across the bridge the gap had been covered with planks, which could be removed quickly if the enemy approached.

Lord Fairfax was heavily outnumbered by the approaching Royalist forces, even though he had gathered all his available troops at Tadcaster. This lack of manpower would be a continual problem for the Fairfaxes. In a letter to Parliament he lists his army as having twenty-one companies of foot, seven troops of horse and a company of dragoons, a force of over 2,500 men if it had been anywhere near

The River Wharfe at Tadcaster, looking south over the bridge.

Looking east towards high ground from the bridge. The Parliamentary earthwork was at the top of the hill.

full strength. It is highly unlikely that Lord Fairfax's force ever approached anything like this number, and his son gives a figure of only 900 men, which means that many units would have been well below half strength.

The contemporary accounts give few details of the Royalist forces. Sir Thomas Fairfax states that the Royalist army marched south from Newcastle with 6,000 men, and this could be a very close estimate. The surviving Yorkshire forces, which had not marched south with the King, had been joined to the Earl of Newcastle's north-eastern troops, and a substantial garrison left in York. The Duchess of Newcastle writes that her husband had advanced with 'his foot and cannon, attended by some troops of horse'. Sir Henry Slingsby gives Newport's force a strength of 15,000 horse and dragoons, which is obviously an error, but a figure of 1,500 is probably close to the truth. This force also had two light guns attached to it. It is probable that Newcastle had about 4,000 foot and several hundred horse with him, which tallies with Sir Thomas Fairfax's estimate of 4,000 for Newcastle's attacking force.

Following the decision reached at the council of war the Parliamentary forces prepared to withdraw, but were prevented from doing so by the rapid Royalist advance. Sir Thomas Fairfax describes the opening of the action:

> But before we could all march out the enemy advanced so fast that we were necessitated to leave some Foot in a slight work above the bridge, to secure our retreat. But the enemy pressing still on us, forced us to draw back and maintain that ground.

Leaving a rearguard of musketeers manning the earthwork the Parliamentary army prepared to withdraw, but the Royalists closed on the rearguard in such strength that the main Parliamentary force had to return to support them. The Duchess of Newcastle also intimates that the Royalist attack was pressed hard, writing of her husband that:

Early in the morning [he] appeared before the town on the east side thereof, and there drew up his army, planted his cannon, and closely and orderly besieged that side of the town.

The action seems to have started at sometime between ten and eleven in the morning. The Royalist attack was met by point-blank fire from Fairfax's musketeers. Sir Thomas writes that:

Our men reserved their shot till they were very near, which then, they disposed to so good purpose, as forced them to retire and shelter themselves behind the hedges that were hard by.

Having been driven off by the Parliamentary musketeers, the Royalist foot sheltered behind the hedges close to the earthworks. The battle then continued with an exchange of fire, which lasted almost until nightfall. Once again there is disagreement among the sources about the extent of the fighting, and while Sir Henry Slingsby describes it as 'light skirmishing', Sir Thomas Fairfax writes that the fight continued 'with cannon and muskets without intermission' until nightfall. Lord Fairfax states that the fight continued 'in sharp dispute', and that 40,000 musket and a great number of cannon shot were discharged by both sides.

However sharp the fight around the earthwork was, the Royalists made no further progress. Only in one area did they come close to success. A body of foot had advanced down the river from the north and captured a number of houses close to the road and the bridge, and for a short while they cut off the Parliamentary

In Tadcaster, looking east towards the area of the earthwork.

In the area of the earthwork looking down York Road, along which Newcastle's army approached the town.

musketeers from their support. These houses are almost certainly the ones around the junction of the York road and Mill Lane. Both Sir Thomas and his father describe the fighting for possession of these buildings. Sir Thomas writes:

> They had, once, possessed a house by the bridge, which would have cut off our reserves, that were in the town; but Major General Gyffard with a commanded party, beat them out again; where many of the enemy's were slain, and taken prisoner. They attempted at another place, but were also repulsed by Captain Lyster, who was there slain; which was a great loss, being a discrete Gentleman.

Lord Fairfax also mentions the loss of Captain Lister in his letter to Parliament:

> The enemy had once won part of the town, and beaten out our soldiers, and placed some of their company in two or three houses, which did much endanger us; but in the end our men, with great courage, forced them out again, recovered and burnt the houses, and killed many of the enemy's that were there placed, and, in conclusion, forced the whole army to retreat, leaving many of their men dead, and great numbers wounded. The certain numbers nor qualities of the persons we could not take; but it is generally said by the country people that there were at least 100 found killed and burnt; and we took seventeen prisoners in the fight. And on our part we lost six men, and Captain William Lister, a valiant and gallant gentleman, who was shot with a musket-bullet in the head; and we had about twenty more wounded; and lost not one prisoner in the battle.

Cut off from their supports by the Royalist troops occupying the houses close to the bridge, it is likely that the Parliamentary musketeers in the earthworks would have run low on ammunition and been driven out. Several counterattacks drove the Royalists from the houses, which were set on fire to prevent their reoccupation. During one of these counterattacks Captain Lister was shot and killed.

What had happened to the Earl of Newport while all this was going on? The Parliamentary forces were concentrating on the fighting to the east of the bridge, and now was the ideal time for Newport to strike from the west, which would almost certainly have resulted in a decisive Royalist victory, and possibly the destruction of the whole Parliamentary army. Unfortunately for Newcastle, Newport never appeared. The Duchess of Newcastle gives a dark overtone to Newport's failure to arrive, writing that '(whether it was out of neglect or treachery that my Lord's orders were not obeyed) that day's work was rendered ineffectual as to the whole design'. Drake, in his history of York, attributes Newport's failure to appear to a trick played by Captain Hotham:

> Captain Hotham, at the beginning of the fight, wrote a letter to the Earl of Newport signed 'Will. Newcastle', and sent it by a running footboy to tell him that, though his commission was to come and assist him, yet he might now spare his pains, and stay till he sent him orders the next morning.

If there is any truth in this story then Hotham pulled off a brilliant tactical ploy, but Drake assumes Hotham's knowledge of Newport's flank march, a presupposition that has no evidence to support it. There was probably a much more mundane reason for Newport's absence: the two guns he had with him, and the state of the roads in December, had slowed him so much that he simply never reached the field. This is supported by Sir Henry Slingsby, who states that 'his march was so troublesome having with him 2 Drakes [light cannon] that it grew too late'.

With the fall of night the Royalist army drew back and camped close to the town. The Parliamentarians held the ground they had occupied that morning. During the night a decision was taken to withdraw, Fairfax to Selby and Hotham to Cawood. The Duchess of Newcastle ascribes this withdrawal to 'the vigilancy of my Lord' putting the enemy into 'such a terror'. Once again the real reason is much more mundane – the Parliamentary army had virtually run out of ammunition and powder. Lord Fairfax believed that he could have maintained his ground 'if we had been furnished with powder and shot'. On the morning of 8 December the Royalist army occupied the town. The battle had been a drawn one. Although Fairfax had caused more casualties than his opponent, Newcastle had gained the strategic upper hand.

CHAPTER IV

'The Rider of the White Horse'
– the attack on Bradford
and the storming of Leeds

Let God arise, and then his enemies shall be scattered. Psalm 68

In the aftermath of the Battle of Tadcaster, the Earl of Newcastle moved south to Pontefract, where he garrisoned the castle. He also established a number of smaller garrisons and quarters, which effectively cut Lord Fairfax off from the heartland of his support in the West Riding mill towns, as Sir Thomas Fairfax reports:

> Now the Earl of Newcastle laid between us and our friends in the West Riding, and so, equally destructive to us both. But, to give them encouragement and help; I was sent with about 200 foot and 3 troops of horse, and some arms, to Bradford. I was to go by Ferrybridge, our intelligence being, that the enemy was yet advanced no further than Sherburn [-in-Elmet]: But when I was within a mile of the town, we took some prisoners who told us that the Earl of Newcastle laid at Pontefract. Eight hundred men in Ferrybridge, and the rest of the army in all the towns thereabout. So as, now, our advance and retreat seemed alike difficult; but there being not much time to demur in, a retreat was resolved on, back again to Selby. Three or four hundred of the enemy's horse showed themselves in our rear, without any attempt upon us, and so, through the goodness of God, we got safe thither, and in three days after (having better intelligence how they lay), with the same number as before, I marched in the night, by several towns where they lay, and arrived the next day at Bradford: A town very untenable; but for their good affections, deserving all we could hazard for them.

It was very fortunate for Sir Thomas that he had captured a number of Royalist prisoners. Without the information they provided he would have run into the

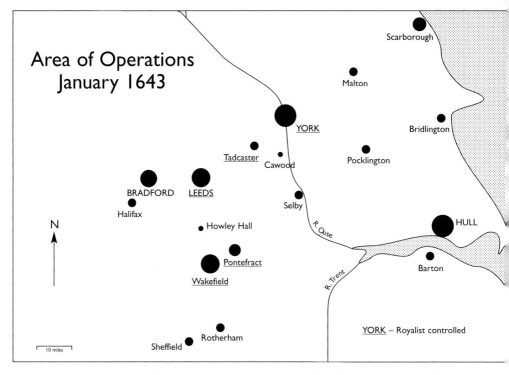

Area of Operations
January 1643

Scarborough

Malton

YORK

Bridlington

Tadcaster
Cawood

Pocklington

BRADFORD   LEEDS

Halifax

Selby

N

Howley Hall

R. Ouse

HULL

Pontefract

Barton

Wakefield

R. Trent

Rotherham

Sheffield

YORK – Royalist controlled

10 miles

garrison at Ferrybridge, which outnumbered him by almost two to one. Having extricated his force from a very tricky situation, he returned to Selby, where he waited for three days before successfully attempting a night march to Bradford. The delay could have been catastrophic for the Parliamentary cause, for Bradford had been attacked.

Having cut Lord Fairfax's army off from its main recruiting area, Newcastle despatched a sizeable force into the West Riding under Sir William Saville, with orders to take Wakefield, Leeds, Bradford and Halifax. If this had been achieved, Fairfax would have been in an unenviable predicament. Before him lay the enemy army, which greatly outnumbered his own, his source of supplies and recruits lost, and an increasingly reticent ally to his rear. In all probability the campaign for Yorkshire would have been over. There is a saying: 'Cometh the hour, cometh the man'. In the case of Bradford it should be 'Cometh the hour, cometh the men', as the ill-armed, and vastly outnumbered, citizens of the town had, beyond all reason, not only held the town, but sent their enemies scurrying back to Leeds in disorder.

Sir William Saville had moved his force into the West Riding, occupying Wakefield and Leeds without a fight, as both had a majority of Royalist sympathisers, which was not the case at Bradford and Halifax. Saville despatched a letter from Leeds to the citizens of Bradford, stating his intention to burn and plunder the town. At nine o'clock on the morning of Sunday 18 December, his army approached the east end of the town, with the intention of carrying out his threat.

Saville's force was split into two parts – an advance guard and a main body. The advance guard was commanded by Colonel Evers, the eldest son of Lord

Evers, and comprised three troops of horse, two companies of dragoons, 100 foot and two drakes (light guns). The main body was commanded by Sir Francis Howard, and was made up of his own and Captain Hilliard's troops of horse, six companies of Colonel Eddington's regiment of dragoons, and 100 foot. The Royalist force totalled almost 1,000 men, and a contemporary anonymously written tract, *The Rider of the White Horse*, referred to in future as the *Rider*, states that they were all Yorkshiremen. The same account also reported Colonel George Goring and the Earl of Newport being with the force, although neither seems to have held a command.

The author of the *Rider* gives a good description of Bradford's defenders:

> I shall now show how our men were marshalled, but it is a hard matter to marshal those who have neither commanders, colours, nor distinct companies. The night before, we had borrowed a commander of Halifax, we had near upon 40 muskets and calivers [a type of musket], in town, about 30 fowling, birding and smaller pieces together with almost twice as many clubmen. These our Captain disposed in several parts of the town, 10 or 12 of our best marksmen upon the steeple, and some in the church; who being next to the enemy, awaited not their warning piece, at the first sight gave fire upon them bravely.

All the trained soldiers that had been raised in Bradford had marched with Lord Fairfax, and remained in Selby with him. Fortunately an officer had arrived from Halifax on the previous day, to take command of the defence. The defenders had about 70 assorted firearms, and twice as many clubmen, giving a strength of about 200 men. The Bradford citizens were armed with a very mixed bag of weapons, ranging from hunting guns to clubs and scythes.

The Royalists were initially taken by surprise, expecting Bradford to surrender as Leeds and Wakefield had. Recovering quickly, and realising how important the church was to the defence of the town, they quickly occupied several houses close to it, which provided shelter for their men, and a good position for their cannon. A troop of horse, commanded by Sir John Goodrick, was despatched to the far, western end of town, and the *Rider* records their activities:

> From thence sent out Sir John Goodrick's troop, who partly to divert us from hindering them planting their cannon, and partly to hinder the parish from coming in to our aid, passed through some parish villages on the one side of the town, robbed a woman, most cowardly slew two naked [unarmed] men, and so came within sight of our sentinel at the west end of the town, our musketeers there discharged at them, shot 2 or 3 horses, whereof one of them lightly wounded was brought into town, and in a short space (partly by our shot, partly by the approach of some clubmen from Bingley) they were forced to retire back to their strength.

Bradford had not been abandoned by the other staunchly Parliamentary mill towns in the area, as is shown by the arrival of the Bingley men, the first of a number of reinforcements to arrive during the day.

Eighteenth-century map of the Leeds/Bradford area from Thomas Jeffreys's The County of York Survey'd, *1775.*

While Goodrick had been diverting attention to the western end of town, the Royalists had deployed several guns, which were used to bombard the church, and to fire down Kirkgate, along which the defenders had to move to reach the church. The commander of the Royalist guns, Major Carew, having successfully deployed them, now decided to take an active part in the attack, leading a body of musketeers to capture a pair of houses within thirty yards of the church. The defenders had been unable to prevent this advance, as they did not have enough men to sally out and attack Carew. There then followed a close-range musketry exchange between the defenders in the church and the Royalists in the houses, the fire being so heavy that the Royalists were unable to send reinforcements forward to relieve their men.

This situation continued until noon when a strong body of reinforcements, comprising a few muskets and a large contingent of clubmen, arrived from Halifax. These immediately reinforced the defenders around the church and in the lanes close to it. The Royalists had failed to take advantage of their numbers, and had attacked the defences on a very narrow frontage, being able to use only a few of their men at a time. The defenders were still in a dangerous position, heavily outnumbered, and with the enemy close to them. They now decided to force the issue, as the *Rider* reports:

> But this was not the way to repel the enemy. The largeness of the church windows, and smallness of the houses, made their assault secure, and our defence dangerous, which our men perceiving, resolved to win or lose all at one; watching for an opportunity between discharge and charge [loading] of the enemy, they sallied out of the church, and being seconded by those in the lanes, rushed in upon the houses, burst open the doors, slew those that resisted, took those who yielded; the rest fled into the next field, whither some few of ours followed, (the greatest part being employed in conveying men [prisoners] and munitions which the enemy had left behind them) and in the field the skirmish was hotter than ever.

One of the Halifax reinforcements, Captain John Hodgson, records the arrival of the news of the attack on Bradford, and the Halifax men's involvement in the attack on the houses close to the church:

A good man, one Isaac Baume, come in haste to Coalley Chapel, and there acquaints the minister, one Mr Latham, what their condition was at

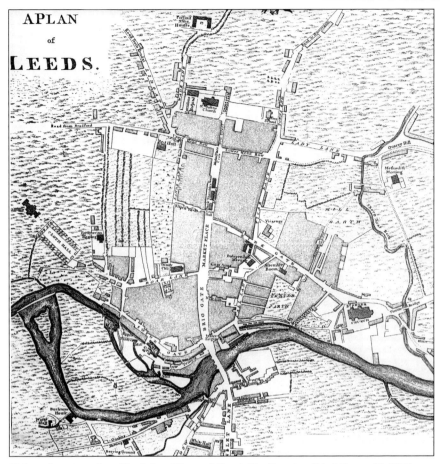

Eighteenth-century plan of Leeds from Thomas Jeffreys's The County of York Survey'd, *1775.*

Bradford; and he enlarged upon it to the congregation, with a great deal of tenderness and affection, so that many of us did put our hands to the plough with much resolution, being well appointed with necessary weapons; and coming down to Bradford Kirk, found the enemy ready to make an attempt upon them in the Kirk. But we gave them no time; but with a party of clubmen, or such as had scythes laid in poles, fell upon their horse on one side, and the musketeers in the houses, that were ready to storm the church, on the other side, and beat them off; took most of them prisoners that were got into the houses; and had taken their guns, but that we wanted a scattering of horse.

At the time Hodgson was a volunteer, although he would remain in arms and achieve the rank of captain in due course. The defenders attacked in a disordered mob, usually a recipe for disaster, but on this occasion it worked to their advantage, as they were so intermingled with the retreating enemy that the Royalist cannon and musketeers were unable to fire on them for fear of hitting their own men. The author of the *Rider* does not seem to have been impressed by the performance of the Royalist troops during the action, but goes on to compliment the courage of their commanders:

> To speak ingenuously, their commanders exasperated by the cowardice of their common soldiers, manifested great courage, but they smarted for it, our scythes and clubs now and then reaching them, and none else did they aim at. One amongst the rest in a scarlet coat, our clubmen had got hold of (and he in all probability, as some credible reports give us occasion to believe, was Colonel Goring) and were spoiling him. Their horse fearing the loss of such a man, became more courageous than they intended, leaped over the hedge, and rode full upon our men, forcing them to give a little ground; too much (alas that they had known him) to lose such a man, but they quickly recovered the ground although they lost the man; doubled their courage, would neither give nor take quarter; (nor was this their cruelty, as the enemy complains, but their ignorance) and in the end forced both man and horse to leave the field.

Goring, battered and bruised, had a lucky escape, if the 'credible reports' are to be believed, although he would gain his revenge on the clubmen at Seacroft Moor several months later (see Chapter 5). A number of Royalist officers were not as lucky as Goring, being cut down as they tried to surrender. One of them may have been the son of the Earl of Newport. The lack of mercy shown by the clubmen gave rise to the term 'Bradford quarter', which meant no quarter! The enemy horse and foot were forced from the field, but this then proved to be a disadvantage to the defenders, as the Royalist musketeers now put down a hail of fire, which caused the Parliamentarians to withdraw to the nearest hedge to take shelter.

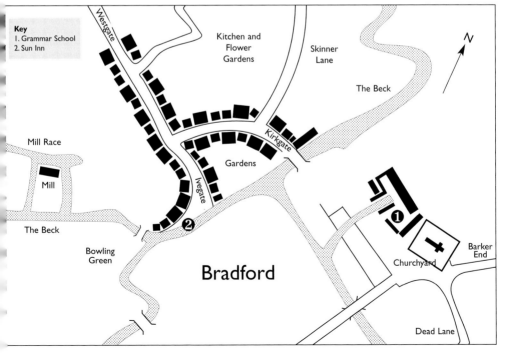

George, Baron Goring (1608–1657)

Born on 14 July 1608, George Goring was the son of the Earl of Norwich. He became famous as one of the most brilliant courtiers at the court of Charles I, but his profligate spending led him to seek employment on the Continent as a soldier. The Earl of Cork, his father-in-law, was induced to purchase Lord Vere's commission in the Dutch service for him, which gave him command of twenty-two companies of foot and a troop of horse, with the rank of colonel. At the siege of Breda in October 1637, he received a wound in the leg, close to the ankle, which left him with a limp for the remainder of his life.

Returning to England to recover from his wound, he was appointed governor of Portsmouth on 8 January 1639. In the 1st Bishops' War Goring commanded a regiment, and continued to build on his growing reputation as a soldier. He then tried to re-enter the Dutch service, but the outbreak of the 2nd Bishops' War saw him in command of a brigade of the King's troops.

In the build up to the 1st Civil War Parliament considered Goring to be a staunch supporter of their cause, and appointed him to the governorship of Portsmouth once again. Parliament was wrong, and Goring obtained money from the Queen to help garrison and fortify the town for her husband's cause. It took some time for Parliament to realise what Goring was up to, and there was even talk of appointing him as lieutenant-general of horse to the Earl of Essex, who was Parliament's senior commander. Early in the 1st Civil War Parliament realised their mistake and blockaded Portsmouth, which was badly fortified and weakly garrisoned, and Goring surrendered the town in early September 1642.

Goring spent the next couple of months in Holland, recruiting officers and veteran troops from among the large number of Englishmen in the Dutch service. He returned to England, with his recruits, in December 1642, when the Earl of Newcastle appointed him general of horse. He quickly showed his calibre by defeating Sir Thomas Fairfax at the battle of Seacroft Moor. On 21 May Wakefield was stormed by the Parliamentarians, and Goring, the Royalist commander, was captured, after rising from his sick bed to lead a counter-attack. At least one contemporary account hints that it was drink, and not illness, that saw him swaying in his saddle during the fight. For the next nine months he remained a prisoner, mainly in the Tower of London. In April 1644 he was exchanged, and rejoined Newcastle's Northern Horse. He commanded Prince Rupert's left wing at Marston Moor, where he swept his opposition away, one bright spot in the Royalists' defeat.

In the aftermath of Marston Moor he marched south with the remnants of Rupert and Newcastle's army. In late 1644 he was appointed to an independent command in the West Country, where his men gained a bad reputation for the depredations they carried out against all and sundry. Following the Royalist defeat he returned to the Dutch service, and then moved on to Spain, where he died in 1657.

Goring was a brave and resourceful soldier, although his love of gambling and debauchery very often had an adverse affect on him. He was ambitious and would stop at nothing to achieve his objective, as the Earl of Clarendon writes: 'His ambition was unlimited, and he was unrestrained by any respect to justice or good nature from pursuing the satisfaction thereof'. Summing up his character Clarendon adds: 'And of all his qualifications dissimulation was his masterpiece'.

While the fighting in the field was in progress, the Royalist cannon continued to fire down Kirkgate and at the church tower. The *Rider* reports that not one ball hit the tower, and although it was crowded with people, not a single casualty was caused in Kirkgate. Three or four houses had been hit by cannon balls, but the only one to suffer any major damage was the house of a Royalist sympathiser.

The Royalists had had enough. Using their horse to cover the withdrawal of their guns and foot, they began their retreat to Leeds, pursued by fifty musketeers and clubmen. The author of the *Rider* writes:

> Which courage in ours, did most of all astonish the enemy; who say, no 50 men in the world, except were they mad or drunk, would have pursued a thousand. Our men indeed shot as they were mad, and the enemy fell as they were drunk, and so we will divide it. Some discharge 10 some 12 times in the pursuit; and having the whole body of the enemy for their butt [target], it may easily be imagined what good execution they did in a miles march.

Once open ground was reached the Parliamentary pursuers returned to Bradford, fearing that the enemy's horse would overwhelm them. It is reported that some of the pursuers were so exhausted after eight hours fighting that they could barely get back to the town. The fact that fifty men were able to pursue the whole Royalist force illustrates how demoralized the Royalists must have been by their repulse. One of the pursuers had a very lucky escape, or so the Rider reports:

> One thing I cannot omit, a hearty Roundhead left by his comrades, environed with the enemy's horse, discharged his musket upon one, struck down another's horse with the thick end [butt] of it, broke a third's sword, beating it back to his throat, and put them all to flight; which (though as the rest wonderful) I dare pawn my credit to be true.

The courage of desperation! The battle was over, and Bradford was safe for the time being. A number of Royalist officers were identified among the dead, along with many unknown common soldiers. Over 100 Royalist wounded returned to Leeds, as was reported to Bradford by a sympathiser living in the town. Major Carew, 26 soldiers, 100 horses, 40 muskets and a large quantity of powder were captured by Bradford's defenders, who had only twelve men wounded, two of whom subsequently died.

Several days after the battle, although the exact date is not known, Sir Thomas Fairfax arrived at Bradford with his reinforcements. Sir Thomas writes of his efforts to put Bradford into a better state of defence:

> Our first work, there, was to fortify ourselves, for we could not but expect strong opposition in it, seeing there laid at Leeds, 1,500 of the enemy; and 1,200 at Wakefield, neither above 6 or 7 miles from us. They visited us every day with their horse (for ours went not far from the town, being so unequal in number) yet they seldom returned without loss; till at length our few men grew so bold and theirs so disheartened, as they dare not stir a mile out of their garrison.

As well as fortifying Bradford, Sir Thomas put a call for volunteers out to the local towns, which was very successful. By 22 January 1643, he had gathered enough men to make an attempt to capture Leeds.

On the morning of Monday 23 January, Fairfax and his force set forth from Bradford. There seem to be some discrepancy between Sir Thomas's account and *The Rider of the White Horse*. Sir Thomas states that he had about 1,200 or 1,300 men, while the *Rider* goes into more detail, stating that the Parliamentary force comprised six troops of horse, three companies of dragoons, almost 1,000

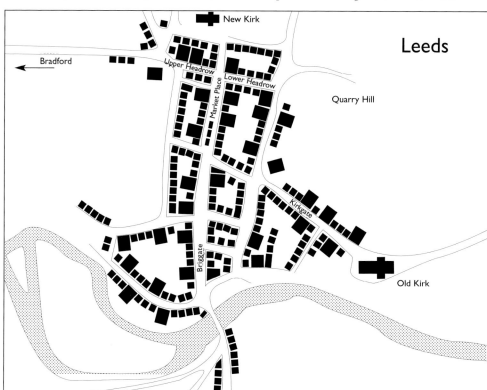

musketeers and 2,000 clubmen. The mounted troops were commanded by Sir Henry Foulis, and the foot by Sir William Fairfax, while Sir Thomas Fairfax had overall command. How can this discrepancy be explained? Firstly, the two sources are almost in agreement about the number of mounted troops and musketeers in the force. Fairfax says that he had 'about 800' foot, and the combined force was 1,200 to 1,300 men strong, while the *Rider* states that there were almost 1,000 musketeers and nine troops/companies of horse and dragoons, giving a strength of between 1,300 and 1,400 men. Where the main discrepancy lies is in Fairfax's omission of the clubmen. He seems to have had a low opinion of their fighting worth, even though they had fought very well while defending their own town a few weeks earlier. He also failed to mention a large force of them that were present at Adwalton Moor in June 1643. So the difference in numbers could have been caused by something as simple as Sir Thomas's lack of esteem for clubmen.

Sir William Saville commanded the Royalist garrison at Leeds, which had a strength of about 1,500 foot, five troops of horse and dragoons, and two demi-culverins, which were large cannon. At the time of the battle, Leeds comprised three main streets: Briggate, the Headrow, and Kirkgate, and all three streets still exist. The top half of Briggate was the Market Place, and the town hall, and several butchers' shops, stood in the centre of the street. The town was well fortified, with the ends of Briggate and the Headrow being barricaded, and having defensive works close to them. A trench ran from close to St John's Church, past the Headrow, and down to the River Aire, which ran along the south edge of the town. At the bottom of Briggate was a bridge across the Aire, hence the street's name, Bridge Gate, and the road ran from there towards Hunslet to the south of the town. The main road from Bradford approached the western end of the Headrow, and it was along this road that Sir Thomas Fairfax's main force approached.

Fairfax had split his force into two parts, the main body approaching Leeds from the Bradford side, while a force of one company of dragoons, thirty musketeers and 1,000 clubmen, under Captain Mildmay, were despatched to Hunslet, where they approached Leeds from the south-east. This force had two tasks: firstly, to attack Leeds across the Aire bridge and up Briggate; and secondly, to prevent messengers from Sir William Saville to the garrison of Wakefield taking the direct route.

As Sir Thomas approached the end of the Headrow he sent a trumpeter into the town to summon Sir William Saville to surrender it 'for the use of King and Parliament', and Sir Thomas writes of Saville's reply:

> They presently returned this answer, that it was not civilly done to come so near the town before I sent the summons, and that they would defend the town the best they could with their lives.

With his summons rebuffed, Sir Thomas began his attack at about two o'clock. Initially, he sent five companies of his best foot, commanded by Sergeant-Major Forbes, south towards the river, skirting the enemy trenches, which were about six feet wide and high. These musketeers, and those commanded by Sir Thomas Fairfax at the western end of the Headrow, then became involved in a protracted

Looking down the Headrow in Leeds towards Bradford, the direction from which the Parliamentary force approached.

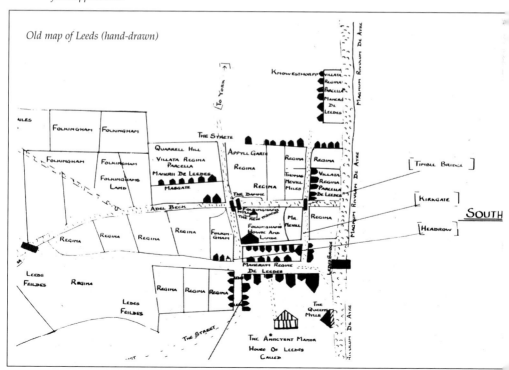

Old map of Leeds (hand-drawn)

musketry exchange with the defenders. At the same time Sir William Fairfax led several companies of musketeers around the north side of the town, and began to put pressure on the defenders close to St John's Church.

On the south side of the Aire, Captain Mildmay's troops approached the town along the road from Hunslet, and the *Rider* mentions their attack on the outer defences:

> Approaching the bridge, [they] forced the guards to quit the works at the first sentry, placed on the outside of the houses towards Beeston, broke through the works, and shot at the other strong sentry at the bridge end, where the forts discharged upon them without any loss to either side, but seeing the very near approach of the dragoons, musketeers and many clubmen and fearing the speedy forcing of that place, they instantly fetched to the bridge the demi-culverin.

By this time, Sergeant-Major Forbes and his men had been involved in a bloodless exchange of musketry for about an hour. Mildmay's men realised that if they could get some musketeers across the fields to the river bank, they could flank the enemy musketeers engaged with Forbes and force them from the works, allowing Forbes's men to break into the town. A number of Mildmay's men took it upon themselves to advance in ones and twos towards the river, the first forward being a dragoon called James Naylor. In due course half a dozen men made it to the riverbank, and took shelter in a narrow lane and behind a tree stump. They were spotted, and the

Looking up the Headrow towards the Royalists' barricade.

Looking down Briggate through the old Market Place. Several buildings stood in the centre of the street at the time of the battle. The Parliamentary attacks converged at this point.

Kirkgate looking towards the Old Kirk (St Peter's).

cannon near the bridge opened fire on them, with little effect. The *Rider* describes the effect that these brave half-dozen had on the enemy defenders:

> About 4 muskets from the little lane, and 2 from under a stump of a tree, a little above by the waterside, discharged amongst the sentry, and one man being there slain, the rest perceived their error, and in conclusion fled apace out of the lower sentry, which being espied by those on the south side of the Aire (Sergeant-Major Forbes and his company not discerning them, for the height of their works hindered) a great shout from those on the south side of the water, discovered it to the Sergeant-Major, who with his forces coming down towards the waterside was helped by Lieutenant Horsfall, who lending him his shoulder to climb to the top of the works, he most furiously and boldly entered the works single, his said Lieutenant [Horsfall] (wading through the riverside below the works) next followed most resolutely, then the rest followed.

Among the men following Forbes into the enemy works was a Mr Schofield, the minister of Crofton Chapel near Halifax, and he led the men in singing the first verse of Psalm 68: 'Let God arise, and then his enemies shall be scattered, and those that hate him flee before him'.

As the Parliamentary men entered the works, and burst into song, another shout went up from their comrades on the south side of the river, informing them that the enemy, about 100 men, had abandoned the next work, which Sergeant-Major Forbes immediately entered, while Mr Schofield led the men in the next verse of the psalm! The defenders had now been driven from their works at the south end of Briggate, and Forbes and Mildmay's men began to fight from house to house, winkling the defenders out as they went. The second demi-culverin was positioned further up Briggate, to defend the street, but Mr Schofield, not only a man of prayer, but also a man of action, led twelve musketeers up Briggate to capture it, killing the gunners in the process.

The defenders began to abandon their posts throughout the town, and Sir William Saville, after trying to rally a body of his men, offered to lead them forward himself, which offer they turned down by taking to their heels, joining in the rout, and almost being drowned trying to swim the Aire. The barricade at the western end of the Headrow had been cleared by this point, and Sir Thomas Fairfax led his troops of horse in a charge up the Headrow and into the Market Place at the top of Briggate, where he met Forbes and Mildmay's men coming up the hill. Sir Thomas sums up the assault very briefly:

> So presently ordering the manner of the storm, we all fell on at one time. The business was hotly disputed for almost two hours. But after the enemy were beaten from their works, the barricades were soon forced open to the streets, where horse and foot resolutely entering, the soldiers cast down their arms, and rendered themselves prisoners. The governor and some chief officers swam the river and escaped.

Although giving only a brief account of the action, Captain John Hodgson is very much in agreement with Sir Thomas and the author of the *Rider*:

Briggate looking towards the Aire bridge. Captain Mildmay's troops approached the bridge from the far side (Hunslet).

> Sir Thomas drew us down into the bottoms towards Leeds, and by degrees we entered the town near the waterside, and our horse broke in on the other side, and met in the market place and beat out their horse and foot, and put them all to run.

By four o'clock the town had been taken. The defenders had lost between forty and fifty killed, and 460 common soldiers as prisoners, along with a number of officers. The Parliamentarians had also captured fourteen barrels of gunpowder, the two demi-culverins, a large quantity of match, and many muskets. Parliamentary losses had been minimal.

The survivors of the Leeds garrison arrived at Wakefield at about six o'clock in the evening, and their arrival seems to have spread panic among the garrison of that town. Wakefield was abandoned during the night, and the garrison withdrew to Pontefract. A Parliamentary force from Almondbury, near Huddersfield, comprising 200 musketeers and 1,400 clubmen, under captains Birkhead and Wilson, occupied Wakefield on 24 January. The consequences of the storming of Leeds went well beyond the occupation of the town, taking of prisoners, and capture of material, as Sir Thomas reports:

> But the consequence of this action was, yet, of more importance; for those that fled from Leeds and Wakefield (for they also quitted that garrison) gave my Lord Newcastle such an alarm, where he lay at Pontefract, as he drew all his army back again to York; leaving once more a free intercourse between my father and us, which he had so long cut off.

The taking of Leeds and Wakefield had opened up communications between Sir Thomas and his father at Selby. Sir Thomas would remain in the West Riding until he was called back to Selby at the end of March.

CHAPTER V

'The greatest loss we ever received'
– the Battle of Seacroft Moor

The balls were whistling upon me in such style that you may easily believe I loved not such music. Queen Henrietta-Maria

In the aftermath of the loss of Leeds and Wakefield,Newcastle and his army returned to York. Before he could turn his attention once again to Lord Fairfax, Newcastle had two tasks to carry out. The first was to send General James King, with a body of horse, to escort an ammunition convoy from Newcastle to York. King had recently been appointed as Newcastle's Lieutenant-General, replacing the Earl of Newport, who had failed to carry out his orders at the Battle of Tadcaster. On 1 February this convoy was intercepted by a force from the garrison of Scarborough, commanded by Sir Hugh Cholmley, at Yarum Bridge (Yarm) in North Yorkshire. The Duchess of Newcastle briefly describes the action:

> A convoy of horse that were employed to conduct it from thence, under the command of the Lieutenant-General of the Army, the Lord Ethyn [King became Lord Eythin after the Royalist victory at Adwalton Moor – see Chapter 7], was by the enemy at a pass, called Yarum Bridge, in Yorkshire, fiercely encountered; in which encounter my Lord's forces totally routed them, slew many, and took many prisoners, and most of their horse colours, consisting of seventeen cornets [horse standards]; and so marched on to York with their ammunition, without any other interruption.

It would seem that the forces involved were two sizeable parties of horse, although few further details are to be found. It is a fair assumption that General King had a substantial body of horse to escort an important convoy. Although Cholmley's force would have been smaller than King's it could still have numbered up to 800 men, if the capture of seventeen cornets is to be believed. Even with the advantage of terrain Cholmley's force was badly beaten, and this defeat could have been instrumental in his defection to the Royalist cause in late March:

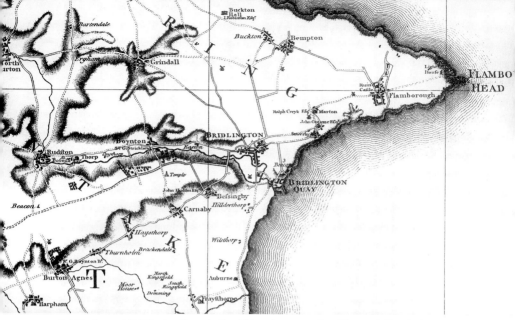

Bridlington and Bridlington Quay in the eighteenth century, from Thomas Jeffreys's The County of York Survey'd, *1775.*

> Not long after, my Lord, who always endeavoured to win any place or persons by fair means, rather than by using of force, reduced to his Majesty's obedience a strong fort and castle upon the sea, and a very good haven, called Scarborough Castle, persuading the governor thereof, who heretofore had opposed his forces at Yarum Bridge, with such rational and convincible arguments, that he willingly rendered himself, and all the garrison, unto his Majesty's devotion.

So the Duchess of Newcastle writes. She also sums up the importance of Cholmley's defection:

> By which prudent action my Lord highly advanced his Majesty's interest; for by that means the enemy was much annoyed and prejudiced at sea, and a great part in the East Riding of Yorkshire kept in due obedience.

But that was in the future. Newcastle still had to contend with the Queen returning from Holland to a hostile coast. With this in mind he decided to attack Malton, which lay between York and the coast, and was garrisoned by the Parliamentarians, who fell back rapidly to Hull. News was brought to Newcastle of the Queen's arrival at Bridlington, while he was at Pocklington. Having driven the enemy back to Hull he turned his army towards the coast.

The Queen had landed on 22 February, and remained at Bridlington awaiting the arrival of Newcastle's army. On the morning of the 24th several Parliamentary warships hove into view and commenced a bombardment of the town and the ships in the harbour. Queen Henrietta-Maria described the events that followed in a letter to King Charles:

God, who took care of me at sea, was pleased to continue his protection by land, for that night, four of the Parliament ships arrived at Burlington [Bridlington] without our knowledge, and in the morning [24 February], about four o'clock, the alarm was given that we should send down to the harbour to secure our ammunition boats, which had not yet been able to be unloaded; but, about an hour after, these four ships began to fire so briskly, that we were all obliged to rise in haste, and leave the village to them: at least the women, for the soldiers remained very resolutely to defend the ammunition. One of the ships had done me the honour to flank my house, which fronted the pier, and before I could get out of bed, the balls were whistling upon me in such style that you may easily believe I loved not such music. Everybody came to force me to go out, the balls beating so on all the houses, that, dressed just as it happened, I went on foot to some distance from the village, to the shelter of a ditch, like those at Newmarket; but before we could reach it, the balls were singing round us in fine style, and a sergeant was killed twenty paces from me. We placed ourselves then under this shelter, during two hours that they were firing upon us, and the balls passing over our heads, and sometimes covering us with dust. At last, the Admiral of Holland [Admiral van Tromp] sent to tell them, that if they did not cease, he would fire upon them as enemies. On this they stopped, and the tide went down, so that there was not water enough for them to stay where they were. I am told that one of the captains of the Parliament ships had been before hand to reconnoitre where my lodgings was, and I assure you that it was well marked, for they always shot upon it.

Shortly thereafter Newcastle's army arrived at Bridlington, and escorted the Queen back to York, where she arrived on 7 March. As mentioned previously, a combination of his defeat at Yarm Bridge and the Queen's safe arrival seems to have finally prompted Sir Hugh Cholmley to turn his coat, and declare for the King, on 25 March. This defection was a great boon to the Royalists, as Scarborough and its garrison gave them control of a large swathe of the East Riding, a safe haven, and control of much of the east coast of Yorkshire.

Cholmley's defection seems to have had an affect on the Hothams. They began a correspondence with the Earl of Newcastle with the intention of changing sides, and became increasingly uncooperative with Lord Fairfax. Later in the year, in the aftermath of the Battle of Adwalton Moor (see Chapter 7), the Hothams would try to seize control of Hull, but were prevented from doing so by the town's citizens. Both father and son would later face Parliament's retribution on Tower Hill.

Lord Fairfax found himself adrift at Selby with little support. Newcastle's main army was at York, Cholmley was in control of much of the East Riding, and the Hothams had withdrawn their troops into Hull. Fairfax's power base lay in the West Riding among the textile producing towns, Leeds, Bradford and Halifax in particular. The West Riding also had direct connections into Lancashire, where Manchester and Bolton held many staunch supporters of Parliament, and might be able to provide him with troops. Sir Thomas Fairfax sums up his father's predicament:

For being now denied help and succour from Hull and the East Riding, he was forced to forsake Selby, and retire to Leeds and those western parts

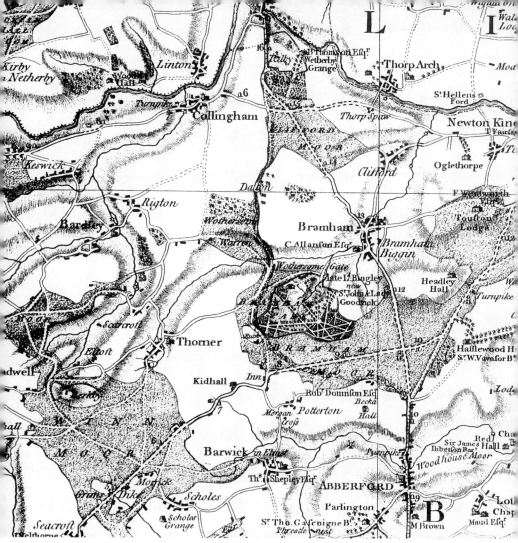

The area between Tadcaster and Seacroft, from Thomas Jeffreys's The County of York Survey'd, *1775.*

where myself was. But to make good this retreat, I was sent to bring what men I could, to join with him at Sherburn; for Newcastle's forces lay so as he might easily intercept us in our way to Leeds, which he had determined, and to that end lay with his army on Clifford Moor, having perfect intelligence of our march.

This was a very dangerous manoeuvre to carry out – a march across a prepared enemy front – particularly when outnumbered. Sir Thomas returned from the West Riding with a small force of horse and musketeers, supplemented by a large body of clubmen: local volunteers armed with whatever they could find. He was tasked with providing a diversion for his father's march by attacking the small garrison at Tadcaster.

On the morning of 30 March, while his father marched towards Leeds along the line of the modern A63, Sir Thomas moved north towards Tadcaster. He would have followed the route of the modern A162, which runs from Sherburn-in-Elmet to Tadcaster, and at the time of the battle was part of the Great North Road, now replaced by the A1. His march took him through a small village called Towton. On the fields to the south of the village, and west of the road, the bloodiest battle of the Wars of the Roses took place on Palm Sunday in 1461. If medieval chroniclers are to be believed, it could be the largest and bloodiest battle fought on British soil, although modern historians tend to revise down the number of combatants considerably. At the north end of Towton the road continues towards Tadcaster, but at the time of the Civil Wars it turned sharply left and descended into the valley of the Cock Beck. Now all that is left of the original road is a dirt track, which runs down the side of the Rockingham Arms public house. Sir Thomas, and his men, would have crossed the Cock Beck on a small bridge, a modern version of which still exists. Here is the site of the 'bridge of bodies' where, according to the medieval chronicles, the stream could be crossed dry shod by stepping on the bodies of the routed Lancastrian soldiers after the Battle of Towton. There is also a very good chance that King Harold Godwinson crossed the bridge with his army in 1066, on his way to defeat the Norwegians at the Battle of Stamford Bridge, and on his return to London prior to the Battle of Hastings.

Tadcaster was garrisoned by 3–400 men, who promptly abandoned the town on the approach of Sir Thomas's force. Newcastle had planned to send a large body of horse to intercept Lord Fairfax's march, but the attack on Tadcaster gave him pause for thought. He feared that his intelligence had been incorrect, and that rather than marching to Leeds Lord Fairfax was actually advancing on York. With this in mind, Newcastle deployed his whole army in order of battle on Clifton Moor. Sir Thomas's diversion had worked very well, and now was the time for him to cut and run, while the Royalists were unsure of what was happening. If he had withdrawn his force at this point they would, in all probability, have arrived safely at Leeds. Yet rather than withdrawing, Sir Thomas writes that his men 'stayed 3 or 4 hours slighting the works'. There seems to be little reason for this, although Captain John Hodgson, one of Sir Thomas's officers, gives a possible explanation:

> And Sir Thomas, exceeding his commission at the request of the club-men, he marches to Tadcaster to pull down their works, and there trifles out time so long, until horse and foot were marched over at Thorpe Arch, and got near our way when we retreated.

This statement may point to the fact that Sir Thomas's original orders may not have been to attack Tadcaster, but to demonstrate towards it. Finding the town empty, he may have been persuaded to destroy the Royalist earthworks before marching on to Leeds. It is difficult to understand why Sir Thomas delayed, but by the time he began his withdrawal a large force of Royalist troops had crossed the River Wharfe at Thorpe Arch, to the north of Tadcaster, and was advancing rapidly towards him.

The Royalist force was commanded by Colonel George Goring, an excellent but erratic cavalry commander. Although Hodgson writes of 'horse and foot', both Sir Thomas Fairfax and the Duchess of Newcastle speak only of horse and dragoons. Sir Thomas states that Goring had twenty troops of horse and dragoons, which would have given a force of about 1,000 men. It is difficult to ascertain how many of this force were dragoons, but they probably made up a very small proportion of the whole.

Sir Thomas's force was probably slightly larger than Goring's, although its composition would cause Sir Thomas major problems in the ensuing action. He had only three troops of horse, about 150 all told. The remainder of his force was made up of foot, musketeers and clubmen. The Duchess of Newcastle writes that 800 prisoners were captured, and as Fairfax's horse broke on first contact, by far the bulk of these prisoners would have been from his foot. Add to this the number slain in the battle, 'many that were slain in the charge' according to the Duchess, and the odd lucky few who escaped the field, and it gives an approximate total of 1,000 for Fairfax's foot soldiers. Once again it is difficult to ascertain what proportion of this force were clubmen, although Sir Thomas writes of the effect that the capture of such a large number of men had on the economy of the West Riding towns, and this may indicate that the clubmen formed a large part of his force.

Sir Thomas had a major tactical problem on his hands. He had to carry out a fighting withdrawal against an opponent that was vastly superior in horse, across two large areas of open ground: Bramham Moor and Winn Moor. The part of Winn Moor closest to Seacroft village was known as Seacroft Moor, hence the name of the battle. A very good 18th-century map exists of the area of the action. It is part of Thomas Jeffreys's *The County of York Survey'd*, which was published in 1775. Sir Thomas Fairfax gives the most detailed account of the action, and the terrain he describes fits closely with that shown on Jeffreys's map.

The Parliamentary troops began their march up on to Bramham Moor, closely pursued by the Royalist horse. Sir Thomas takes up the story:

> We were newly drawn off when he came. Goring passed over the river to follow us; but seeing we were so unequal to him in horse (for I had not above three troops, and to go over Bramham Moor, a large plain) I gave directions to the foot to march away while I stayed with the horse to interrupt the enemy's passage in those narrow lanes that led up to the Moor. Here was much firing one at another; but in regard of their great number, as they advanced, we were forced to give way, yet had gained by it sufficient time for the foot to be out of danger.

Using the narrow lanes to offset his numerical inferiority, Fairfax intended to hold the Royalists up long enough for his foot to reach the cover of the enclosures between Bramham Moor and Winn Moor. Fairfax doesn't mention hand-to-hand fighting, but does mention a lot of carbine and pistol fire. If Goring's horse outnumbered Fairfax's so greatly, why did he not use his superior numbers to charge and defeat the Parliamentarians? The lanes he was advancing up were narrow and bordered by high, thick hedges, and in their narrow confines only

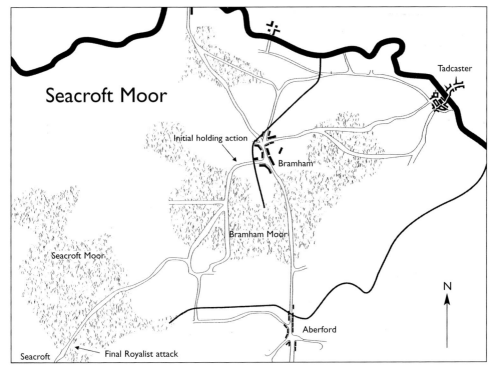

Seacroft Moor

Tadcaster

Initial holding action

Bramham

Bramham Moor

Seacroft Moor

N

Aberford

Seacroft

Final Royalist attack

limited numbers of men could face each other. On his day Goring was an astute tactician, although prone to bouts of drunken debauchery, and he did not want to be drawn into an equal battle. It is very likely that he deployed his dragoons, in a dismounted role, to move through the enclosures and outflank Fairfax's troopers. Rather than receive close-range fire into his flank, Fairfax would have pulled his men back. The process could then be repeated.

Sir Thomas continued his steady withdrawal until he believed he had given his foot enough time to cross Bramham Moor. Imagine his surprise when he discovered his foot had not moved! He writes:

> But when we came up to the Moor again, I found them where I left them, which troubled me much, the enemy being close upon us, and a great plain yet to go over.

It is understandable that Sir Thomas was 'much troubled'. The enemy was approaching and a decision had to be made, so he divided his foot into two divisions and set them off across the Moor, protecting their rear with his three troops of horse. The Royalists had by now deployed onto the Moor in three equal bodies and continued to shadow the Parliamentary withdrawal, keeping within a few hundred yards, 'about two musket shots' as Sir Thomas noted. It is difficult to understand why Goring did not attack as Fairfax crossed Bramham Moor. With hindsight it can be said that his decision was a sound one, and his delaying the attack until the enemy was crossing Seacroft Moor was wholly justified.

Upon reaching the enclosures between Bramham Moor and Winn Moor Sir Thomas must have heaved a sigh of relief, but things were about to get worse:

But having again, gotten to some little enclosures, beyond which was another moor, called Seacroft Moor, (much less than the first) here our men thinking themselves more secure, were more careless in keeping order, and while their officers were getting them out of the houses where they sought for drink, (being an exceeding hot day), the enemy got, another way, as soon as we, upon the Moor.

These houses were probably the village of Kidhall, and Jeffreys's map shows an inn in the village where the road emerges from the moor, so it may be that some of Fairfax's men were not only looking for water to drink. Sir Thomas states that Goring's force had got onto the moor by another route, and such a route is clearly shown on Jeffreys's map, passing through Thorner.

The crisis point of the battle was now approaching. As Fairfax's column emerged from the enclosures onto the moor, Goring's men shadowed them a few hundred yards to the north. The Parliamentarians had almost reached the safety of Seacroft village when Goring turned his men into line and charged, and with 1,000 horse bearing down on them Fairfax's men stood little chance. Sir Thomas describes this attack and its results:

> But when we had almost passed this plain also, they seeing us in some disorder, charged us both in flank and rear. The Countrymen presently cast down their arms and fled; and the foot soon after, which, for want of pikes were not able to stand their horse. Some were slain, and many taken prisoner. Few of our horse stood the charge. Some officers, with me made our retreat, with much difficulty, in which Sir Henry Foulis had a slight hurt. My cornet was taken prisoner, yet got to Leeds about 2 hours after my Father and the forces with him had arrived thither safe.

Faced with such an onslaught the Parliamentary forces fell into disarray. The clubmen seem to have fled immediately, while the remainder of the foot, the musketeers, put up a slightly better showing. Once they had discharged their muskets they had little protection against the enemy horse, having few, if any, pikemen present. Heavily outnumbered, Fairfax's horse seems to have decided that discretion was the better part of valour, and left their foot to it. Most of the horse seems to have escaped but few of the foot soldiers did, the vast majority being captured or slain. Captain Hodgson is very much in agreement with Sir Thomas:

> Our poor foot suffered much, but the horse escaped to Leeds. I was there sore wounded, shot in two places, cut in several, and led off, into a wood, by one of my soldiers, called Killinghall wood. With much ado he got me to Leeds in the night, and it was a considerable time before I was cured.

The Parliamentarians had been well and truly beaten. The Duchess of Newcastle states that 800 prisoners were taken, along with many killed. As has already been mentioned, the loss of these men had a major effect on the economies of a number of West Riding towns. Trying to gain prisoners to exchange for the men captured at Seacroft Moor was a major reason for the Parliamentary attack on Wakefield, which is discussed in the next chapter. Sir Thomas Fairfax summed up the Battle of Seacroft Moor as 'the greatest loss we ever received'.

Chapter VI

'A Miraculous Victory'
– the storming of Wakefield

And truly for my part I do rather account it a miracle, than a victory.

Ferdinando, Lord Fairfax

After their defeat at Seacroft Moor the Fairfaxes concentrated their troops into two main garrisons at Leeds and Bradford. It was shortly after this that one of the most enigmatic battles of the Civil War in Yorkshire took place at Tankersley near Barnsley. The Duchess of Newcastle writes:

> Immediately after, in pursuit of that victory [Seacroft Moor], my Lord sent a considerable party into the west of Yorkshire, where they met with about 2,000 of the enemy's forces, taken out of their several garrisons in those parts, to execute some design upon a moor called Tankerley Moor, and there fought them, and routed them; many were slain, and some taken prisoners.

With a 'considerable party' on one side and 2,000 men on the other, the action at Tankersley was far from a skirmish, but contemporary accounts tell nothing more about it. An unpublished local history in Barnsley Library gives a few more details, saying that the Parliamentary forces came north from Derbyshire and were commanded by one of Sir John Gell's brothers, Sir John being Parliament's commander in Derbyshire. They were met and defeated by a large force of Royalists led by Sir Francis Wortley. The account states that the action took place between Tankersley Church and Harley, and if this is correct the M1 south of junction 36 bisects the battlefield. Several artefacts, mainly cannonballs, have been ploughed up close to Tankersley Church, and at one time were held there. Unfortunately, the local historian who provides the additional detail does not give his sources, so it is difficult to prove the veracity of his account.

Newcastle now decided that it was time to clear a route for the Queen to begin her march south with the convoy of arms and ammunition for the King. His initial intention was to take Leeds and Wakefield, but having spent several days in an abortive siege of Leeds he moved his army south to Wakefield, where he left a garrison of 3,000 men before moving into the south of the county. First he marched to Rotherham, to which he laid siege. The Duchess of Newcastle describes the subsequent events:

> My Lord first marched to Rotherham, and finding that the enemy had placed a garrison of soldiers in that town, and fortified it, he drew up his army in the morning against the town, and summoned it; but they refused to yield, my Lord fell to work with his cannon and musket, and within a short time took it by storm, and entered the town that very night; some enemies of note that were found therein were taken prisoners; and as for the common soldiers, which were by the enemy forced from their allegiance, he showed such clemency to them, that very many willingly took up arms for his Majesty's service, and proved very faithful and loyal subjects and good soldiers.

Lord Fairfax puts a very different perspective on the events at Rotherham in a letter to William Lenthall, the Speaker of the House of Commons, written in Leeds on 23 May:

> The Forces in Rotherham held out two days siege and yielded up the Town upon treaty, wherein it was agreed, that the Town should not be plundered, and that all the Gentlemen Commanders and Soldiers (six only excepted, that were specially named) leaving their Arms, should have free liberty to go whither they pleased; But when the enemy entered, contrary to their Articles, they have not only plundered the Town, but have also made all the Commanders and Soldiers, prisoners, and do endeavour to constrain them to take up Arms on their party.

There are a number of major discrepancies between these two accounts. How long did Rotherham hold out? Was it taken by storm or treaty? What happened to the prisoners? One possible explanation is that the town was summoned and refused to submit, which then prompted an abortive assault by Newcastle's forces. On the following day the defenders, realising the desperation of their situation, came to an agreement. The rules of war at the time said that if a town was summoned and refused to surrender, and an assault had to take place, then the town would be subject to sacking if it subsequently fell. Newcastle's men probably thought it was their right to plunder the town after they had been forced to assault it, and Newcastle and his officers may not have had a lot of say in the matter. Whether this explanation is correct or not, Rotherham fell on 4 May.

Two days after the fall of Rotherham, on 6 May, Newcastle moved his army towards Sheffield. Both Royalist (the Duchess of Newcastle) and Parliamentary (Lord Fairfax) accounts reported that the garrison abandoned both the town and castle, which were occupied on the same day by the Royalists. On 9 May Newcastle installed Sir William Saville as the governor of the town, with orders to begin production of cannon at the local ironworks. Newcastle then seems to have spent a couple of weeks bringing the rest of South Yorkshire under his control. On 21 May he received startling news – Wakefield had fallen to the Parliamentarians, along with the bulk of its garrison.

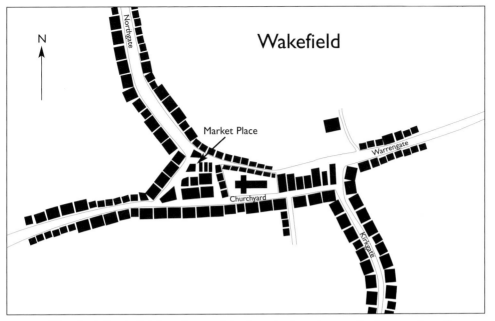

Why had Lord Fairfax chosen this time to launch an attack on a heavily garrisoned town? One obvious reason is that Newcastle and his main army were some distance away in the south of the county, but his son gives another reason for the attack – gaining prisoners for exchange:

> Being most busied about releasing of prisoners that were taken at Seacroft Moor, most of them being Countrymen, whose wives and children were still importunate for their release (and which was earnestly endeavoured by us, but no conditions would be accepted) so as their continual cries, tears and importunities compelled us to think of some way to redeem these men; so as we thought of attempting Wakefield (our intelligence being that the enemy had not above 8 or 900 men in the town).

As will be seen, the Fairfaxes' intelligence services were very wrong in their estimates of the strength of Royalist garrison. Prisoner exchange was a regular event at the time but the Parliamentarians had few prisoners to exchange. If they captured Wakefield and its 900-man garrison they would be able to organise an exchange for the prisoners taken at Seacroft Moor. This may not seem a very convincing reason to attack an enemy garrison, but the loss of 800 men at Seacroft Moor had a major effect on the area's economy. Most of these prisoners were from the Bradford and Halifax areas, and both these towns had populations of around 1,000. It can be seen from this that the loss of 800 military-age men would have had a substantial effect on the region, and redeeming them became a matter of priority.

The Parliamentary plan was to attack Wakefield during the early hours of the morning of Whitsunday, 21 May 1643. The attack force would be commanded by Sir Thomas Fairfax, and would gather at Howley Hall, near Batley, by midnight on the Saturday. This force would be gathered from the garrisons of Bradford, Leeds, Halifax and Howley Hall itself, and would comprise 1,500 men. In a report written by Sir Thomas and several other senior officers after the assault, their force is given as 1,000 foot, eight troops of horse, and three troops of dragoons. If Lord Fairfax's reported total of 1,500 men is correct then each troop of horse and dragoons would have numbered approximately forty to fifty men. The horse was divided between Sir Thomas Fairfax and Sir Henry Foulis, each having four troops, while Sergeant-Major General Gifford and Sir William Fairfax commanded the foot. No account speaks of the Parliamentary force having any artillery, which is hardly surprising as their mission was to surprise a lightly defended town.

Sir Thomas's first target was a small Royalist garrison at Stanley, which comprised two troops of horse and some dragoons. Arriving at about two o'clock in the morning Fairfax quickly scattered the Royalist horse, capturing twenty-one prisoners in the process.

The Parliamentary force then continued on to Wakefield, where some delay ensued as the force split and moved into position to attack Northgate and Warrengate simultaneously. Alerted by the remnants of the troops quartered at Stanley, Royalist musketeers and horse awaited the attack, as is reported by Sir Thomas and his officers:

> About four a clock in the morning we came before Wakefield, where after some of their horse were beaten into the town, the foot with unspeakable courage, beat the enemies from the hedges, which they had lined with musketeers into the town.

Upon news of the attack on Stanley, the Royalists had manned the hedges and barricades with musketeers, and had sent a patrol of horse out towards Stanley. These were quickly driven back into the town by the approaching Parliamentarians. Five hundred Royalist musketeers had also been deployed outside the town, manning the hedges of the surrounding fields, and once again these troops were driven back into the town. At this stage Sir Thomas began to get a niggling doubt about the size of the garrison. Having encountered so many men outside the town he began to suspect that the initial estimate of 8–900 men might be a little low, and consequently he called his officers together for a short conference. It was decided that the attack should continue.

The plan called for an assault on the works at two separate points, at the ends of Northgate and Warrengate. Wakefield, and many other towns attacked during the Civil Wars, should not be thought of as a fortified town, with walls and earthworks, as at Newark for example. The main defences of Wakefield were the hedged enclosures, which most houses in the town had. These presented a substantial obstacle to enemy foot, and prevented entry into the town by horse. The ends of each street were barricaded, and a combination of the barricades and hedges made for formidable defences. The major drawback was the narrowness of the barricades at the street ends, which would restrict the number of defenders able to deploy to defend them at any given time.

Although no contemporary accounts state which Parliamentary troops attacked at which point, it can be surmised that Sir Thomas and Gifford attacked down Warrengate. There are two reasons for supposing this. Firstly, their force was the

Wakefield Cathedral. Parliamentary troops planted a captured gun in the churchyard to bombard the Royalist troops in the Market Place, beyond the buildings in the lower left of the photograph.

first to reach the Market Place, and it is a much shorter distance from the end of Warrengate to the Market Place than from the end of Northgate. Secondly, Gifford planted a gun in the churchyard to fire on the Royalist troops gathered in the Market Place. The church is close to the end of Warrengate, and anyone attempting to reach the church from Northgate had to cross the Market Square, which was packed with enemy troops.

The Royalist defences seem to have held for some time, with contemporary accounts talking of between one and a half and two hours before the Parliamentary troops managed to break in. Interestingly, Sir Thomas Fairfax was involved in writing both of these accounts. The first was written shortly after the attack, the second not until after the Civil Wars, and where it differs from the first account the earlier work will be used. Both assaults seem to have broken into the town at about the same time, and Sir Thomas describes the attack along Warrengate:

> After 2 hours dispute the foot forced open a barricade where I entered with my own troop. Colonel Alured and Captain Bright followed with theirs. The street which we entered was full of their foot which we charged through and routed, leaving them to the foot which followed close behind us. And presently we were charged again with horse led by General Goring, where, after a hot encounter, some were slain, and himself [Goring] taken prisoner by Captain Alured.

Warrengate looking towards the cathedral. George Goring was captured leading a counter-attack along the street.

This account in Fairfax's post-war memoirs is very much in agreement with that written by him and his officers soon after the action:

> When the barricades were opened, Sir Thomas Fairfax with the horse, fell into the town, and cleared the street where Colonel Goring was taken, by Lieutenant Alured, brother to Captain Alured, a Member of the House.

The two accounts are a little confusing regarding the ranks of the Alured brothers. Sir Thomas's later account gives their subsequent ranks, colonel and captain, while the second account gives their ranks at the time of the action, captain and lieutenant. Having captured the barricade at the end of Warrengate, Gifford's men turned one of the artillery pieces they had captured on the Royalists in the street beyond. This allowed them to open the barricade, clearing the way for Fairfax's four troops of horse: Fairfax's, Bright's and the two Alureds', to charge down the street through the Royalist foot, which would be dealt with in turn by Gifford's musketeers. Having cleared the Royalist foot, Fairfax's troops were then struck by a counter-attack led by George Goring, which was beaten off, with Lieutenant Alured capturing Goring in the process. After repulsing this counter-attack, Fairfax's men seem to have become scattered in their pursuit, and Sir Thomas found himself alone:

And here I cannot but acknowledge God's goodness to me this day, who being advanced, a good way single, before my men, having a Colonel and a Lieutenant Colonel (who had engaged themselves as my prisoners) only with me, and many of the enemy now between me and my [men] I light on a regiment of foot standing in the Market Place. Thus encompassed, and thinking what to do, I spied a lane which I thought would lead me back to my men again; at the end of this lane there was a corps du guard of the enemy's, with 15 or 16 soldiers which was, then, just quitting of it, with a Sergeant leading them off; whom we met; who seeing their officers came up to us. Taking no notice of me, they asked them what they would have them do, for they could keep that work no longer, because the Roundheads (as they called them) came so fast upon them. But the gentlemen, who had passed their words to be my true prisoners, said nothing, so

A Miraculous

V I C T O R Y

Obtained by the Right Honorable, FERDINANDO Lord FAIRFAX, against the Army under the Command of the Earl of NEWCASTLE, at WAKEFIELD.

IN

Y O R K - S H I R E :

Of the Enemy there was taken prisoners, Generall *Goring*, Sir *Thomas Bland*, 2 Colonells, Sergeant Major *Car*, 13 Captains, 1500 Souldiers, 27 Colours of Foot, 3 Cornets of Horse, 4 Lieutenants, 15 Ensignes, and 1 Cornet, 4 peeces of Ordnance, all their Ammunition, and a great number of Armes, with the losse of 7 common Souldiers.

Sent in two Letters to the Honorable, W: LENTHALL, Esq; *Speaker in the House of* C O M M O N S.

Also a *LETTER* of great consequence, which was found in Generall *Gorings* chamber, which was sent to him by his Father the Lord *Goring*.

O*Rdered by the Commons in Parliament, That publique Thanksgiving be too morrow, the 28. of this instant May, given in all the Churches and Chappels of London, Westminster, Borough of Southwark, Suburbs and places adjacent for the great and good successe it hath pleased G O D to give the Forces under the Command of the Lord* Fairfax, *at the taking in of* Wakefield ; *And that the Letters relating that good successe, be read in the said Churches and Chappels.*

H: Elsynge, Cler. Parl. D. Com.

M A Y 27. Printed for *Edw.* Husbands. 1643.

Contemporary tract announcing the 'Miraculous Victory' at Wakefield.

looking upon one another, I thought it not fit, now, to own them as so, much less to bid the rest to render themselves prisoners to me; so, being well mounted, and seeing a place in the works where men used to go over, I rushed from them, seeing no other remedy, and made my horse leap over the works, and so, by good providence, got to my men again.

Sir Thomas's personal bravery is beyond doubt, but his common sense, on occasion, can be questioned. Getting cut off from his men seems to have become a habit, and he repeated the feat at Selby and again at Marston Moor in 1644.

While Fairfax was extricating himself from among the enemy, Gifford had continued the attack up Warrengate, bringing the captured cannon with him. When he reached the Market Place he found a large body of enemy formed and awaiting him, and this is mentioned in the report of the Parliamentary commanders:

Yet in the Market Place there stood three troops of horse, and Colonel Lampton's Regiment [foot], to whom Major General Gifford sent a trumpet with offer of quarter, if they would lay down their arms, they answered they scorned the motion; then he fired a piece of their own ordinance upon them, and the horse fell in upon them, beat them out of the town.

Sir Thomas, in his memoirs, writes that Gifford deployed the cannon in the churchyard. Having given the enemy an opportunity to surrender, Gifford opened fire upon them with the cannon and his musketeers, and then he ordered Fairfax's rallied horse to charge them. This was the last straw and the remaining Royalist troops either fled, if they could, or surrendered. By nine o'clock Wakefield, and its garrison, were firmly in Parliamentary hands.

It is difficult to ascertain casualties for either side. Although no figure is given among the contemporary accounts for Royalist losses, Lord Fairfax reported to Parliament that 'in taking the town we lost no man of note, and not above seven men in all', but he does go on to state that 'many of our men were shot and wounded'. His forces captured a large amount of men and equipment: thirty-eight named officers, 1,500 common soldiers, four cannon, twenty-seven foot colours and three horse cornets, along with weapons, and large amounts of powder, ball and match.

It is difficult to see how Fairfax's men had carried out such a feat, capturing a town held not by the 900 men expected, but by 3,000 foot, in six regiments, and seven troops of horse. They had taken a town held by twice their own number, and captured a larger number of prisoners than they had men in their attacking force! There are a number of reasons why this happened. They attacked the town from two points, at its narrowest parts, and as the Royalist commanders sent reinforcements to the endangered barricades, they had no room to deploy and merely queued up in the streets behind. As these troops were driven back into the town, the reserves in the Market Place could not effectively counter-attack the enemy penetrations. In fact this reserve seems to have done nothing other than wait for the enemy to attack them. The Royalist commanders do not seem to have reacted well to the rapidly changing situation, and Dr Nathaniel Johnstone, a contemporary who left behind a wealth of anecdotes, may supply a possible reason:

> There was a meeting at Heath Hall upon the Saturday, at a bowling, and most of the officers and the governor were there, and had spent the afternoon in drinking, and were most drunk when the town was alarmed. It was taken fully by nine o'clock in the morning, and more prisoners were taken than the forces that came against it. It seems probable that Sir Thomas Fairfax had notice of their festivities at Heath, and perceived the advantage which they might afford him.

So, were the Royalist commanders all under the influence of drink when Fairfax attacked? With his subsequent record, it is easy to imagine George Goring leading his men in a charge down Warrengate, swaying in his saddle. Whatever the reason, Sir Thomas Fairfax had taken the town, and his father succinctly sums up the victory:

> And truly for my part I do rather account it a miracle, than a victory, and the glory and praise to be ascribed to God that wrought it, in which I hope I derogate nothing from the merits of the Commanders and Soldiers, who every man in his place and duty, showed as much courage and resolution as could be expected from men.

Sir Thomas's men counted their spoils, before withdrawing to their garrisons. The Fairfaxes had their prisoners for exchange, but how would Newcastle react? They would not have long to wait.

CHAPTER VII

'A wild and desperate man'
– the Battle of Adwalton Moor

*It is resolved on both sides to give battle
and yet neither knew of the other's intention.* Sir Henry Slingsby

In the event, Newcastle's reaction to the storming of Wakefield was far from what the Fairfaxes expected. Assuming that Newcastle would immediately return to Wakefield, Sir Thomas Fairfax gathered his prisoners, and the arms and ammunition captured, and withdrew his men to their garrisons. Instead of striking rapidly at the enemy, Newcastle tamely withdrew his army to York. Once again his secondary mission, the protection of the Queen, seems to have dictated the course of events.

While Lord Fairfax awaited Newcastle's reaction, he wrote a letter to William Lenthall, the speaker of the House of Commons, on 23 May, complaining about the state of his army:

> This overthrow has much enraged the enemies, who threaten a present revenge, and are drawing all their forces this way to affect it. I perceive there are succours sent to Lincolnshire and other adjacent countries [counties], which if they were here, might be employed to as much advantage for the public safety, as in any place. I desire our condition may be seriously thought on by the House, and the aids often promised, may presently march away to join us, and that Colonel Cromwell, with his horse and foot may also be ordered to march to me, that being joined together, I may be able to draw this army into the field, and gain fresh quarter for the soldiers, and furnish ourselves with powder, arms, and ammunition, which is now grown very scarce, and cannot be supplied, until the passage to Hull be forced open, which is now possessed by the enemy. If such succours come not timely to us, we cannot long subsist, but must be forced to accept dishonourable conditions; which besides the loss and ruin of this county, will be a great disadvantage to the general safety,

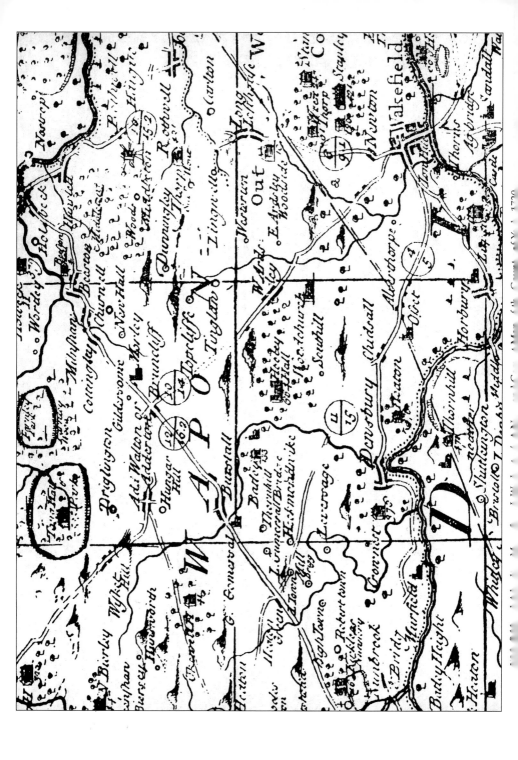

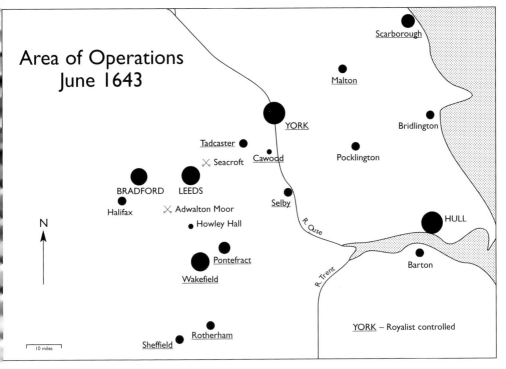

and withal, some course must be thought on to furnish some large proportion of money to defray the soldiers' arrears.

Fairfax felt aggrieved that money and equipment were being sent to other areas where little fighting was taking place, while his own men remained unpaid and ill-equipped. The attack on Wakefield had achieved its primary objective, the taking of prisoners, and while the Fairfaxes awaited Newcastle's next move, a prisoner exchange was arranged.

On 4 June Newcastle and his army, accompanied by the Queen, marched from York to Pontefract. During a stay at the town of several days, a council of war was called, and Sir Henry Slingsby writes of its deliberations:

> Now the Queen was preparing to march to the King, and his excellency [Newcastle] with his army conveyed her to Pontefract, where his excellency caused a council of war to be held, that advice might be taken which was the most useful service in the army, whether to march up with the Queen and so join with the King, or else with the army to stay, and only give order for some regiments to wait upon her majesty. If he marched up, his army would give a gallant addition to the King's, but then he left the country in my Lord Fairfax's power, and it might be he should have him march in the rear of him, and join in the Parliament's forces. If he stayed, he might send some forces with the Queen, and yet be able to lay siege to my Lord Fairfax in Leeds, or fight him in the field. Well, this latter was resolved on, of sending some forces only with the Queen, and himself to stay, and to try the mastery with my Lord Fairfax.

A large proportion of Newcastle's army were Yorkshiremen, and many of these did not want to leave the county while Fairfax's forces were still in the field. The Yorkshire gentry's reluctance to leave the county while any enemies remained would become a recurring theme, and Newcastle would lose a possible war-winning opportunity in the months to come because of it. Once the decision had been made, the Queen was despatched, with a strong escort, to Newark, where she arrived safely on 16 June.

Newcastle spent several days at Pontefract after the Queen's departure, recruiting and training troops to replace those sent south with the Queen. A decision had been taken to advance towards the heart of the area controlled by Lord Fairfax, and Bradford was decided on as the target. Between Wakefield and Bradford lay Howley Hall, close to Batley, and this became Newcastle's first objective. Its governor, Sir John Saville, was summoned to surrender on 21 June. In a letter detailing the events up to the end of June 1643, Newcastle outlines the taking of Howley Hall:

> We marched from Pontefract towards Bradford, and in our way thither we summoned Sir John Saville, commander of Howley, to deliver up that house, and lay down his arms so unjustly taken up, who returned an uncivil answer, and that he would keep it despite our forces, whereupon we planted our cannon against that house, and environed it upon Wednesday the 21st of June in the afternoon, and next morning took it by assault, and in it the said commander-in-chief and all his officers and soldiers, about 245, some few whereof were slain, the rest taken prisoner.

The Duchess of Newcastle adds further details:

> And within a short time, viz. in June 1643, took a resolution to march into the enemy's quarters, in the western parts; in which march he met with a strong stone house well fortified, called Howley House, wherein was a garrison of soldiers, which my Lord summoned; but the governor disobeying the summons he battered it with his cannon, and so took it by force. The governor, having quarter given him contrary to my Lord's orders, was brought before my Lord by a person of quality, for which the officer that brought him received a check; and though he resolved then to kill him, yet my Lord would not suffer him to do it saying, it was inhuman to kill any man in cold blood. Hereupon the governor kissed the key of the house door, and presented it to my Lord; to which my Lord returned this answer: 'I need it not', said he, 'for I brought a key along with me, which yet I was unwilling to use, until you forced me to it'.

In this day and age it may seem a little harsh for the commander of a garrison, which refused to surrender, to be killed. Modern historians often write of the atrocities committed throughout the ages when fortified places were stormed. It was an accepted rule of war, at the time of the Civil Wars, that if a garrison was summoned and did not surrender, which would lead to a protracted siege and storming, they could be put to the sword and the place they held, be it a town, castle or house, sacked. Newcastle, being a very honourable man, had no qualms

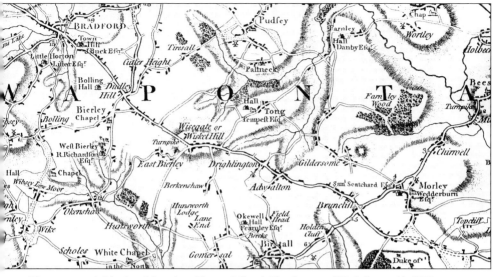

The area around Adwalton Moor, from Thomas Jeffreys's The County of York Survey'd, *1775.*

in ordering a garrison commander's death during an assault, but would not entertain putting him to death in cold blood once he had been taken prisoner.

Newcastle spent the next eight days encamped at Howley Hall, due to heavy rain making the roads all but impassable. On 30 June the Royalists commenced their march to Bradford, little realising that Lord Fairfax's Parliamentary forces were on the same road, attempting to reach Howley Hall and carry out a surprise attack on the Royalist quarters.

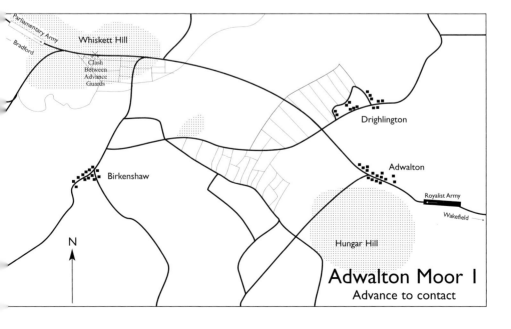

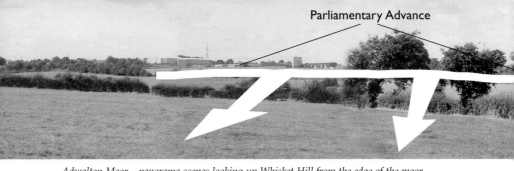

Adwalton Moor – panorama scenes looking up Whisket Hill from the edge of the moor.

In Bradford Lord Fairfax had watched Newcastle's advance into the West Riding, and realised that he had little time to come to a decision. Firstly, he could abandon the West Riding, and attempt to skirt around Newcastle's army and head for Hull, but this was not a very attractive option, as the Hothams were not cooperating with Fairfax – in fact they were very close to changing sides. A second option was to withdraw into Lancashire, towards Manchester, but once again this seems to have been discounted. Another possibility was to stand and defend Bradford, but there were good reasons for not following this course of action, as Sir Thomas Fairfax reports:

> The Earl of Newcastle marched with an army of 10 to 12,000 men to besiege us, and resolved to sit down before Bradford, which was a very untenable place. My father drew all the forces he could spare out of the garrisons hither. But seeing it impossible to defend the town, but by strength of men, and not having above 10 or 12 days provision for so many as were necessary to keep it; we resolved, the next morning very early with a party of 3,000 men, to attempt his whole army as they laid in their quarters, 3 miles off.

To hold Bradford against as large a force as Newcastle had, complete with heavy cannon, would require a lot of men. If Fairfax managed to gather enough men he would only have enough provisions for 10 or 12 days. He was in a real 'Catch 22' situation – he needed a lot of men to defend the town, but couldn't feed them if they came. As Sir Thomas states, this led to a decision being taken to attack the Royalists in their quarters around Howley Hall. Another factor in this decision could well have been the success of the attack on Wakefield, and it is an interesting question whether Lord Fairfax would have decided to attack the Royalists if the attack on Wakefield had not been so successful.

On the morning of 30 June 1643, both armies, unbeknown to each other, were marching along the Wakefield to Bradford road, and Sir Henry Slingsby neatly sums this up:

> It is resolved on both sides to give battle and yet neither knew of the other's intention: they both draw out, his excellency [Newcastle] thinking to find him [Fairfax] within his fortifications; my Lord Fairfax draws out, advancing forwards towards the camp where his excellency lay.

The armies were on a collision course, and would meet close to the village of Adwalton.

The old road between Bradford and Wakefield ran along a narrow ridgeline, running from north-west (Bradford) to south-east (Wakefield). As Lord Fairfax's army marched towards Wakefield, the road began to rise up the north-west side of a hill, known locally as Whiskett, or Westgate Hill, the crest of which stood at about 700 feet. About three quarters of a mile south-east of the main crest of Whiskett Hill was a second crest, slightly lower at 650 feet, which formed the military crest of the hill for an army marching from Bradford. It was not until the top of this hill was reached that Adwalton Moor could be seen, as the ground gently drops into a shallow bowl between the two crests. About half a mile further on was the edge of Adwalton Moor. The north-west edge of the moor had a series of hedged enclosures, and a substantial ditch along it, and further enclosures encroached onto the south-west corner of the moor. A couple of hundred yards from the edge of the moor the land begins to rise again and climbs to 650 feet at the top of Hungar Hill, which formed the south-east edge of the battlefield. On either side of the ridge the ground falls away quite steeply.

As Lord Fairfax's army left Bradford it was divided into a number of bodies. First came the forlorn hope, or advance guard, which was a combined arms force of six companies/troops of horse, foot and dragoons. Although it is not certain what proportion each type provided, it would have had a total of 300–350 men. It was commanded by Captain Mildmay, who seems to have been a trusted officer, more than capable of operating independently, as had been shown at Leeds earlier in the year when he was detached with a substantial force to attack the town from the south side of the River Aire.

The vanguard was commanded by Major-General Gifford and comprised 1,200 men from the Leeds garrison. Lord Fairfax himself commanded the main battle, which was made up of 500 men from the garrisons of Halifax and its surrounding towns, and 700 Lancashire foot, divided into 12 companies. Sir Thomas Fairfax had command of the horse, which was formed from 13 troops, for a strength of about 650–700 men. The horse was divided into two wings of five troops each, which suggests that the remaining three troops were part of the forlorn hope. Thomas Stockdale, a close associate of Lord Fairfax, stated that the Parliamentary army was 'not full 4,000 men horse and foot armed'. Taking into account the troops already listed this gives a total of about 500–600 men for the Bradford garrison, divided into seven companies, which formed the rearguard, commanded by Lieutenant-Colonel Forbes. Thomas Stockdale also mentions a substantial number of clubmen being present, although he does not give an exact number.

The strength of the Royalist army is much more problematic, and little detail is given in any of the contemporary accounts of the battle. Thomas Stockdale stated

Looking back towards the moor from Whiskett Hill. The arrows indicate the line of the Parliamentary advance.

that the Royalists had 15,000 foot and 4,000 horse, almost certainly a highly inflated figure, although his total for the horse may be close. Sir Thomas Fairfax puts the Royalist strength at between 10,000 and 12,000 men, and this is probably very close to the truth. The two Royalist accounts that give any clue to their strength are that of the Duchess of Newcastle, who writes that 'My Lord's forces, which then contained not above half so many musketeers as the enemy had; their chiefest strength consisting in horse', and that of the Earl of Newcastle himself, who reports the enemy as having 'a greater number of foot than we'. It is probable that the Royalist army was nearer in strength to Sir Thomas Fairfax's lower estimate of 10,000 men, with an almost equal split of horse and foot at about 5,000 men each. Newcastle also had a substantial artillery train, as his objective was to lay siege to Bradford.

The first shots of the battle were fired on the north-west slopes of Whiskett Hill, when the two forlorn hopes clashed with one another. No contemporary account gives a time for this first clash, but Sir Thomas Fairfax provides a clue:

> My father appointed 4 o'clock the next morning, to begin to march; but Major-General Gifford, who had the ordering of the business, so delayed the execution of it, that it was 7 or 8 before we began to move; and not without much suspicion of treachery in it.

If Sir Thomas is correct, and the Parliamentary army had covered four miles, then the first clash must have been between nine and ten o'clock, on the morning of 30 June 1643.

Looking up Whiskett Hill. Beyond the road sign were the enclosures fought over by both armies.

Parliamentary Advance

Three accounts give details of the initial clash between the forlorn hopes. Sir Henry Slingsby writes:

> The fortune [forlorn] hope of his excellency's army met unexpectedly with the van of the enemy. They skirmish and are put to retreat. He encouraged his men and put the enemy to a stand. They come on fiercer, and beat the enemy from one hedge, from one house to another; at last they are driven to retreat and we recover the moor.

Thomas Stockdale reported:

> Upon Atherton [Adwalton] Moor they planted ordnance, and ordered their battalia, but they manned diverse houses standing in the enclosed grounds between Bradford and Atherton Moor with musketeers, and sent out great parties of horse and foot by the lanes and enclosed ground to give us fight. Our forlorn hope beat back the enemy's out of the lanes and enclosed ground, killing many and taking some prisoners.

Finally, Sir Thomas Fairfax writes:

> For when we were near the place we intended, the whole enemy army was drawn up in battalia. We were to go up a hill to them, which our forlorn hope gained by beating theirs into their main body, which was drawn up half a mile further, upon a place called Adderton Moor [locals still sometimes refer to Adwalton as Adderton]. We being all up the hill drew into battalia also.

Looking across the lower slope of Whisket Hill. The Parliamentary army drove Royalist musketeers back through this area. The Parliamentary army advanced from left to right.

Parliamentary Advance

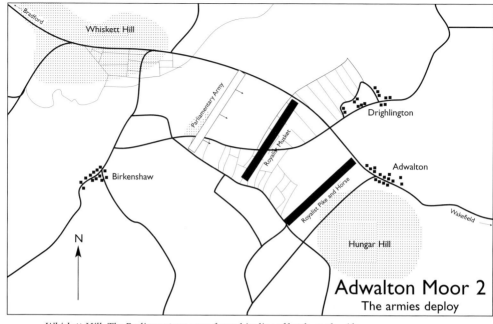

Whiskett Hill. The Parliamentary army formed its line of battle on the ridge.

There seems to be some discrepancy in these accounts about the state of the Royalist army at the start of the action. Enough information is given to work out the course of events.

Captain Mildmay led his forlorn hope up the north-west side of Whiskett Hill, where they clashed unexpectedly with the Royalist vanguard. The Royalists were driven back from Whiskett Hill to the second, lower ridge, where they were rallied by the Earl of Newcastle, and the Parliamentary forlorn hope was brought to a stand. Reinforced, the Parliamentarians renewed their attack, driving the Royalists back into the enclosures at the foot of the hill, and here once again the Royalists made a stand.

By this time the Royalist army had begun to deploy onto the moor, and a large number of musketeers, supported by horse, had been sent into the enclosures to reinforce their retreating forlorn hope. The main Parliamentary army had reached the top of the lower crest, overlooking the moor, and began to form into line of battle. There would have been a pause while both armies continued to deploy.

The Parliamentary army split into two wings and a reserve. Major-General Gifford commanded the left wing, with his five troops of horse deployed close to the Bradford-Wakefield road, and to their right 1,200 foot, mostly musketeers. Continuing the line was a similar sized body of foot, while another five troops of horse completed the Parliamentary line. The right half of the Parliamentary front line was commanded by Sir Thomas Fairfax. Somewhere within this line were deployed three light cannon, the only guns Lord Fairfax had with him. The remainder of Lord Fairfax's troops formed a reserve, and this comprised about 600 regular foot, possibly the men from the Bradford garrison and the clubmen, and, as they are not taken into account elsewhere, Captain Mildmay's weary forlorn hope.

On the moor the Royalists were in the process of deploying into a similar formation, with horse on the flanks and foot in the centre. As most of Newcastle's musketeers had been deployed into the enclosures on the edge of the moor, the foot in the centre would have comprised, in the main, blocks of pikemen, which would have been interspersed with cannon, most of which were still in the act of deploying onto the moor. The troops of horse on the Royalist left flank had problems deploying due to a number of coal pits dotted around the southern half of the moor, and remains of these can still be detected today. The Royalist right flank may well have extended beyond the Bradford-Wakefield road, which was open ground at the time of the battle, but any advance they made would have been affected by a continuation of the enclosures bordering the moor. It is difficult to ascertain how far forward on the moor the Royalists had deployed, but as several accounts write of the Royalists coming down towards the Parliamentary troops, and Parliamentary troops going up towards the Royalists, it is a fair assumption that the main Royalist line was deployed part way up the north-west slope of Hungar Hill.

Once their deployment was complete the Parliamentary army began to roll forward towards the enclosure at the bottom of the hill. After a sharp fight the Royalist musketeers were driven from the enclosures, withdrawing towards their main body, and the Parliamentarian troops closed up to the edge of the moor. Sir Thomas Fairfax's five troops of horse had occupied an enclosure running along the south-west edge of the moor, and some of his musketeers were deployed in

Royalist Pike, Horse and Guns

Panorama looking towards Royalist lines.

another enclosure at right-angles to the first. The only entrance to the field in which Sir Thomas's horse were deployed was through a narrow opening, or gateway, which was flanked by his musketeers, the whole forming a very useful defensive position, and Sir Thomas needed this since the enemy horse opposing him vastly outnumbered his five troops. It was not long before a body of Royalist horse began to move forward to attack him, sweeping around the end of the enclosure to force an entry through the gateway. Sir Thomas reports the results of this attack:

> Ten or 12 troops of horse charged us in the right wing. We kept the enclosure, placing our musketeers in the hedges in the moor, which was a good advantage to us who had so few horse. There was a gate, or open place to the moor, where 5 or 6 might enter abreast. Here they strove to enter, and we to defend; but after some dispute, those that entered the pass found sharp entertainment; and those that had not yet entered, a hot welcome from the musketeers that flanked them in the hedges. All, in the end, were forced to retreat, with the loss of one Colonel Howard, who commanded them.

The Duchess of Newcastle gives similar details to Sir Thomas, but states that the gateway would only allow access to two men at a time. Outnumbered two to one, the importance of Sir Thomas's position is proved, and his men not only held their position, but also drove the enemy off.

Shortly after the repulse of the first cavalry attack, another large body of Royalist horse descended the hill, and almost succeeded in breaking into the enclosure, as Sir Thomas Fairfax reports:

> The horse came down again and charged us, being about 13 or 14 troops. We defended ourselves as before, but with much more difficulty, many having gotten in among us; but were beaten off again, with loss; and Colonel Herne who commanded that party was slain. We pursued them to their cannon.

Panorama looking towards Parliamentary lines from the Royalist lines.

Sir Thomas goes on to describe an act of divine retribution, which took place just after this attack:

> And here, I cannot omit a remarkable passage of divine justice. While we were engaged in the fight with the horse that entered the gate, 4 soldiers had stripped Colonel Herne naked, as he laid dead on the ground (men still fighting around about him), and so dextrous were these villains, that they had done it, and mounted themselves again before we had beat them off. But after we had beaten them to their ordnance (as I said) and now returning to our ground again, the enemy discharged a piece of cannon in our rear; the bullet fell into Captain Copley's troop, in which these 4 men were; two of them were killed and some hurt, or mark remained on the rest, though dispersed into several ranks of the troop which was the more remarkable, we had not martial law among us, which gave me a good occasion to reprove it, by showing the soldiers the sinfulness of the act, and how God would punish when man wanted power to do it.

It is quite a surprise that after ten months at war the Parliamentary army in Yorkshire does not seem to have had any articles of war (regulations governing discipline in the armed services) in place.

The Parliamentarians were exerting pressure right along the line, and began to advance onto the moor itself, driving the Royalist musketeers before them. Joseph Lister, an inhabitant of Bradford, writes that the Parliamentary foot:

> Charged them so warmly, that they beat them off their great guns, and turned them against the enemy and they began to run.

There is no evidence to support Lister's mention of the Royalist guns being captured and turned on their original owners, but several other accounts talk of Fairfax's foot almost reaching the Royalist guns. Sir Henry Slingsby reports that: 'There the enemy had like to have gained our cannon; but was manfully defended by a stand of pikes.' The Duchess of Newcastle said that:

> In the meanwhile the foot of both sides on the right and left wings encountered each other, who fought from hedge to hedge and for a long

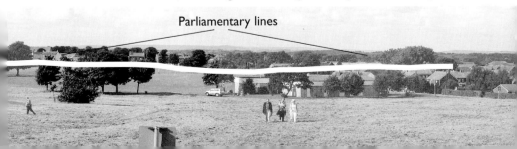

Parliamentary lines

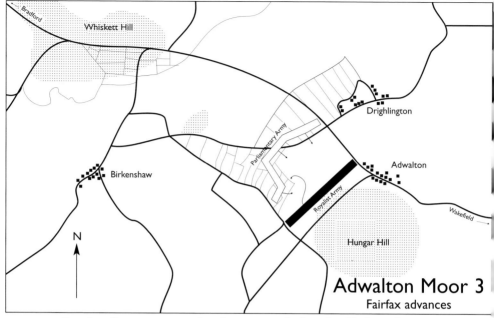

Adwalton Moor 3
Fairfax advances

time together overpowered and got ground of my Lord's foot, almost to the environing of his cannon.

By this time the action had been going on for two hours, and it must have been around noon. The Royalist musketeers had been driven back to their gun line, and the horse of their left wing had been driven back twice by Sir Thomas Fairfax's men. The Royalist right wing does not seem to have taken a great part in the action, and their guns were in danger of capture. Sir Philip Warwick sums up the Royalist situation:

> When the day seemed lost on his side [Newcastle's], and many of his horse and foot standing doubtful and wavering; a stand or body of pikes, which being not useful, where the two armies were strongest engaged, came up to the defence of their foot, and charged by Fairfax's horse, repelling them, gave leisure to rally horse and foot.

Sir Thomas Fairfax takes this a little further:

> This charge and the resolution that our soldiers showed in the left wing, made the enemy think of retreating. Orders were given for it, and some marched off the field.

Outnumbered almost three to one, the Parliamentary army was on the verge of winning a stunning victory. Although the intervention of some of the Royalist pikes had halted the enemy's advance temporarily, the Royalist army was in some disarray, and Newcastle issued orders to withdraw. Battles can sometimes swing on the actions of one man, and Adwalton Moor was a prime example of this. A

Royalist colonel changed the whole course of the action, as Sir Thomas Fairfax reports:

> While they were in this wavering condition, one Colonel Skirton, a wild and desperate man, desired his General [Newcastle] to let him charge once more, with a stand of pikes, with which he broke in upon our men, and not relieved by our reserves, commanded by some ill affected officers, and chiefly, Major-General Gifford (who did not his part as he ought to have done) our men lost ground; which the enemy seeing, pursued their advantage by bringing on fresh troops. Ours being herewith discouraged, began to flee, and so were soon routed.

This turn of events is also mentioned by the Duchess of Newcastle:

> At last the pikes of my Lord's army having had no employment all the day, were drawn against the enemy's left wing, and particularly those of my Lord's own regiment, which were all stout and valiant men, who fell so furiously upon the enemy, that they forsook their hedges, and fell to their heels.

Colonel Skirton, who was probably Colonel Posthumous Kirton, requested Newcastle's permission to carry out one last attack against the enemy, and this turned the course of the battle. Closing rapidly with the enemy musketeers, Kirton's pikemen broke in among them and drove them back into the enclosures. Other bodies of foot joined in this attack, and the situation of Lord Fairfax's left wing deteriorated rapidly. Sir Thomas Fairfax states that Gifford was responsible

Looking from the library car park towards Whiskett Hill.

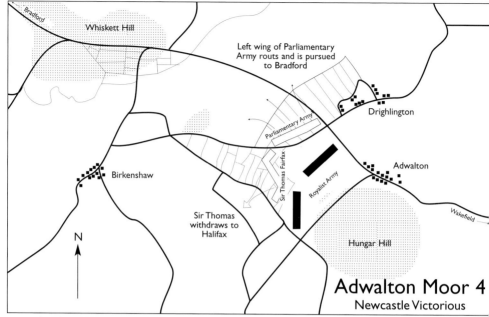

Adwalton Moor 4
Newcastle Victorious

for the defeat, as he failed to deploy the reserve promptly. This hardly seems justified. It was no more Gifford's responsibility to deploy the reserve than it was Sir Thomas's, and his statement seems to be trying to find a scapegoat for the officer whose responsibility it was – his father, Lord Ferdinando Fairfax.

With the enemy forced back into the enclosures, General King, Newcastle's Lieutenant-General, led forward the horse of the Royalist right wing. This was the last straw for Fairfax's left wing, and in short order they were streaming back towards Bradford, with the Royalist horse in full pursuit. Due to the lie of the land, and the mass of powder smoke blowing across the battlefield, Sir Thomas Fairfax was unaware of the disaster on the left flank. Newcastle now turned his attention to Sir Thomas's men, the only surviving formed bodies of Parliamentary troops on the battlefield. The Duchess of Newcastle writes:

> At which very instant my Lord caused a shot or two to be made by his cannon against the body of the enemy's horse, drawn up within cannon shot, which took so good effect, that it disordered the enemy's troops. Hereupon my Lord's horse got over the hedge, not in a body (for that they could not), but dispersedly two on a breast; and as soon as some considerable number was gotten over, and drawn up, they charged the enemy, and routed them. So that in an instant there was a strange change of fortune, and the field totally won by my Lord.

Sir Thomas mentions the enemy guns opening fire on his men as they withdrew to the enclosure they had so stoutly defended, and this continued once they had arrived there. The reason for Sir Thomas's withdrawal was almost certainly the repulse of Gifford's men by Kirton's attack, and finding his men facing the whole Royalist left wing, he had no option but to pull back. Sir Thomas goes on to describe the closing moments of the battle:

> The horse also charged us again. We not knowing what was done in the left wing, our men maintained their ground, until a command came for us to retreat having scarce any way now to do it; the enemy being almost round about us, and our way to Bradford cut off; but there was a lane in the field we were in which led to Halifax, which, as a happy providence, brought us off without any great loss, saving one Captain Talbot and 12 more which were slain in this last encounter.

So there is a discrepancy between the Duchess's account and Sir Thomas's. The Duchess asserts that Fairfax was driven from the field, while Sir Thomas states that he withdrew from the field after receiving an order, probably from his father. Sir Thomas's story has the ring of truth about it, as he brought virtually all of his men off the field in good order, something he certainly would not have been able to do had he been driven from the field. Local tradition has it that the lane along which Sir Thomas withdrew is Warren Lane, which still exists today, although it follows a slightly different course, and passes through the grounds of Oakwell Hall, just to the south of the battlefield.

By early afternoon the Fairfaxes were in full retreat: Sir Thomas to Halifax, and the remainder of the army towards Bradford. Accounts of both sides' losses in the

The first commemorative stone.

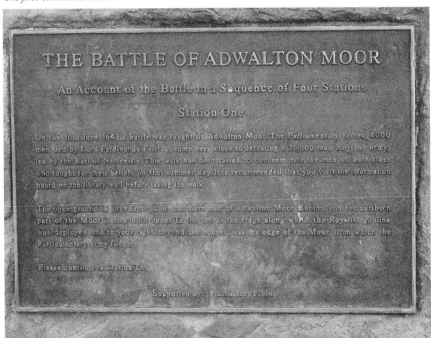

Foot regiment with muskets on the flanks and pike in the centre. Courtesy of John Wilson

battle are sparse and contradictory. For example, Sir Thomas Fairfax puts the Parliamentary losses at 'about 60 killed, and 300 taken prisoners', while the Duchess of Newcastle writes:

> In this victory the enemy lost most of their foot, about 3,000 were taken prisoner, and 700 horse and foot slain, and those that escaped fled into their garrison at Bradford, amongst whom was also their General of Horse [Sir Thomas Fairfax].

Both of these accounts were written a long time after the battle and give vastly different figures, one too low, and one too high. A third account gives more realistic figures, is attributed to the Earl of Newcastle, and was written soon after the battle:

> So we pursued them, killing and taking them to Bradford town end, which was more than two mile [old English miles, nearer four modern miles], in which chase was slain (as is supposed) about 500 of the enemy's, and about 1,400 taken prisoners, amongst which many officers, together with three field pieces, and all their ammunition there, which was not much. We had many soldiers hurt, two colonels of horse slain, Heron and Howard, and some officers hurt, as Colonel Throckmorton, Colonel Carnaby, and Captain Maison, all recoverable, and not above twenty common soldiers slain.

This account gives more reasonable figures for the Parliamentary losses, although the figure for the Royalist dead seems a little low. That said, most of the Parliamentary dead would have been killed during the pursuit after the battle. With the enemy in rout Newcastle was able to continue his march to his original objective – Bradford.

CHAPTER VIII

'Pity poor Bradford'
– the aftermath of Adwalton Moor and the fight at Selby

What a dreadful night was that in which Bradford was taken!
What weeping and wringing of hands! Joseph Lister

With the bulk of Lord Fairfax's army in flight, and his son's troops cut off and withdrawing towards Halifax, Newcastle was now free to continue his march towards Bradford, where he established his headquarters at Bolling Hall. Both sides continued their preparations during the night. The Royalists established two batteries close to Bradford church, in preparation for a bombardment the following morning. In the meantime Sir Thomas Fairfax had gathered a small force of men to him at Halifax, and marched to Bradford to reinforce his father. Thomas Stockdale wrote a letter from Halifax to the Speaker of the House of Commons, which detailed Sir Thomas's efforts:

> Only we have got some 20 horse and 200 foot of them to stay with us at Halifax, upon promise to pay them ready money for their entertainment, which otherwise absolutely refused. Sir Thomas is gone himself to Bradford with some horse and foot that brought hither yesterday.

When Sir Thomas arrived at Bradford he found a scene of great confusion. Grave news had reached his father, which Sir Thomas outlined in his memoirs:

> I found my Father much troubled, having neither a place of strength to defend ourselves in; nor a garrison in Yorkshire to retreat to. (For the Governor of Hull [Sir John Hotham] had declared himself, that if we were forced to retreat thither, he would shut the gates against us). But while he was musing on these sad thoughts, a messenger was sent from Hull to let him know that the townsmen had secured the Governor, and if he had any occasion to make use of that place (for they were sensible of the

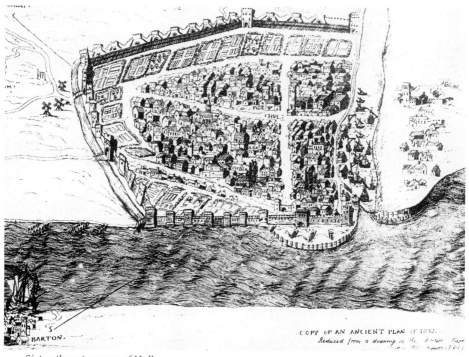

Sixteenth-century map of Hull.

Map of Hull, Wenceslas Hollar, 1640.

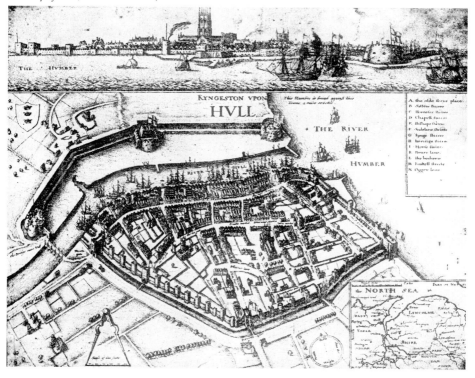

Map of Hull, John Speed, 1610.

danger he was in) he should be readily and gladly received. Which news was joyfully received, and acknowledged as a great mercy of God to us.

The Hothams had continued to connive with the Royalists. Things came to a head on 29 June when Sir John was arrested. He managed to escape but was pursued to Beverley and recaptured. His son had also been arrested, and the pair were taken to London on the ship *Hercules*, and imprisoned in the Tower of London on 15 July. They were both subsequently tried and executed, Captain John on 1 January 1644, and his father on the following day. Although events at Hull seem to have had no connection with the fighting in the West Riding, they could not have occurred at a more fortuitous time for Lord Fairfax. With the arrival of this news he marched to Leeds with the remainder of his army, having left his son with 800 foot and 60 horse to defend Bradford.

The morning of 1 July began with a Royalist bombardment on the town, which paid particular attention to the church. This may seem a particularly barbaric act,

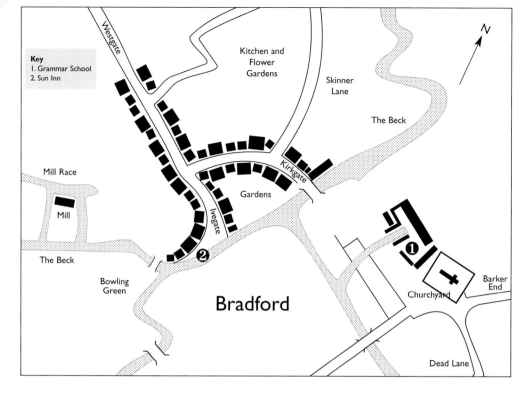

Key
1. Grammar School
2. Sun Inn

Westgate

Kitchen and
Flower
Gardens

Skinner
Lane

The Beck

N

Mill Race

Kirkgate

Gardens

Mill

Ivegate

The Beck

Gardens

②

①

Bowling
Green

Barker
End

Churchyard

Bradford

Dead Lane

but Newcastle explained his reasons in a despatch sent to the King in Oxford:

> The next day we had placed our cannon and made places of batteries very near the town and church, where they had two drakes upon the top of the steeple, and lined the steeple with woolpacks; yet our cannon dismounted their drakes upon the top of the steeple, and battered the steeple so as none could stay on it, where they had many musketeers.

These details are supported by Joseph Lister, who was an inhabitant of the town, and seventeen years old at the time of the siege:

> The enemy was encamped at Bowling [Bolling] Hall; and near the town, on that side of it, they had planted their guns against the steeple, and gave it many a sad shake. The townsmen had hanged woolpacks at that side of the steeple, but the enemy cut the cords with their spiteful shot; and shouted loudly when the packs fell down.

The Royalist bombardment of the church does not seem quite so barbaric when it is realised that the town's defenders had occupied it and put it into a state of defence, even going to the trouble of hoisting two light cannons up the steeple. Why had they done this? The main problem with defending Bradford was that it was overlooked on all sides. Standing in the grounds of Bolling Hall it is easy to see how vulnerable the town was. The cannon in their batteries on the hill could shoot down into the town, while the defenders could not elevate their guns enough to reply, hence raising the drakes to the top of the steeple. Once the defenders had occupied the church it became a legitimate target.

Having given the defenders a taste of what was to come, Newcastle now requested a parley. Sir Thomas Fairfax and Joseph Lister both mention this. Sir Thomas writes:

> Yet notwithstanding the Earl of Newcastle sent a trumpet to offer us conditions; which I accepted, so that they were honourable for us to take, and safe for the inhabitants. Upon which, 2 captains were sent to treat with him, and a cessation during the time. But he continued working, still, contrary to agreement; whereupon I sent for the commissioners again (suspecting a design of attempting something against us) but he returned them not until 11 at night, and then with a slight answer, and while they were delivering it to us, we heard a great shooting of cannon and muskets. All ran presently to the works which the enemy were storming. Here for three quarters of an hour was very hot service; but at length they retreated. They made a second attempt, but were also beaten off. After this we had not above one barrel of powder, and no match.

Joseph Lister gives very similar details:

> But on the Lord's day morning, they beat a drum for a parley, and all that day (during the time of the parley) they spent in removing their great guns just against the heart of the town; so that no way was left for any to escape. There were but few men in the town, and most of their arms and ammunition were lost at Atherton [Adwalton]; they had no match, but what was made of twisted cords dipped in oil. About the going down of the Sun, the parley broke up, and off went their murderous guns before the inhabitants knew, and at the first shot they killed three men sitting on a bench. All that night it was almost as light as day, with the continual firing.

It would seem that Newcastle had no real intention of allowing the defenders of Bradford an honourable way out, using the time that the parley was going on to surround the town and move his men into position to storm it. The Royalist assault continued for about three quarters of an hour, after which time the defenders had little powder or match left. With this in mind Sir Thomas called a council of war, and he and Joseph Lister both report its decisions. Sir Thomas writes:

> So I called the officers together where it was advised and resolved to draw off presently before it was day; and by forcing a way (which we might do they having surrounded the town) to retreat to Leeds.

Joseph Lister adds a few more details, particularly on the predicament of the common soldiers:

> In the dead of the night, the captains were called and a council held, to determine what was best to be done; and it was presently resolved that the

soldiers should be told, they must shift for themselves. The officers were resolved on making a desperate adventure of breaking through the army at the upper end of the town, and all that were willing might forthwith repair thither. But because my Lord had no garrison nearer than Hull, and now no use could be made of their arms for want of match and powder, he would not command the soldiers to go along with him, but leave them to their own choice; for he said they could no longer keep the town.

It must have been a hard decision for Sir Thomas to make, and an even harder one for the poor foot soldiers, who had the choice to surrender or to attempt to break out along with the horse, and possibly face another contested retreat, with another Seacroft Moor as a distinct possibility.

In the early hours of 2 July the breakout attempt began. Sir Thomas's plan seems to have been to attack the enemy lines with a body of foot commanded by a Colonel Rogers, probably carrying all that was left of the powder and match. Once these had cleared the way the remaining troops could withdraw through the gap and head for Leeds. The first part of the plan went well, with Colonel Rogers's command successfully attacking a dragoon quarter. The front of Fairfax's column, about 80 men in all, broke through the gap, but the rear of the column, for whatever reason, turned back and returned to the town. The troops who had broken out seem to have all been mounted men, and Sir Thomas writes in detail about their adventures:

> Myself with some other officers, went with the horse (which was not above 50) by an opener way. Here I must not forget to mention my wife, who ran as great hazards with us in this retreat, as any others, and with as little expression of fear. Not for any zeal or delight (I must say) in the war, but through a willing and patient suffering of this undesirable condition. But now I sent 2 or 3 horsemen before, to discover what they could of the enemy, who presently returned and told us there was a guard of horse close by us. Before I had gone 40 paces (the day beginning to break) I saw them upon the hill above us being about 300 horse. I with some 12 more charged them. Sir Henry Foulis, Major General Gyffard, and myself with 3 more broke through. Captain Mud was slain; and the rest of the horse being close by, the enemy fell upon them, and soon routed them, taking most of them prisoners; among them my wife was, (the soldier behind whom she was, being taken). I saw this disaster, but could give no relief; for after I was got through, I was in the enemy's rear, alone, for those that had also charged through went on to Leeds, thinking I had done so too; but being unwilling to leave my company, I stayed till I saw there was no more in my power to do, but to be made a prisoner with them: Then I retired to Leeds.

Here is another example of Sir Thomas being cut off from his men in the presence of the enemy – it will not be the last! The Earl of Newcastle displayed nothing but gallantry towards Lady Fairfax, initially sending her to York in his own coach, and then, shortly afterwards, returning her to her husband at Hull.

Area around Hull and Beverley from Thomas Jeffreys's The County of York Survey'd, *1775.*

Meanwhile, in Bradford, the remaining defenders and the town's inhabitants awaited their fate. It was widely believed that the dawn would bring another assault, which would almost certainly be followed by a massacre. Joseph Lister awaited the outcome with the remainder of the town's occupants, and he put down on paper his fears and relief when a massacre did not transpire:

> But O! what a dreadful night was that in which Bradford was taken! What weeping and wringing of hands! None expected to live longer than till the enemy came in; the Duke of Newcastle having charged his men to kill all; man, woman, and child in the town, and to give them (Bradford) quarter, for the brave Earl of Newport's sake. However, God so ordered it before the town was taken, that the Earl gave another command, (viz.) that quarter should be given to all. It was generally reported, that on the Lord's day night, something came, and pulled off the clothes of his bed several times, till he had sent out a second order that none should be slain; and then that thing which troubled him went away. This I assert not as fact; but this is a truth, that they slew very few. Some desperate men wounded several, that afterwards died of their wounds, but I think not more than half a score were slain; and that was a wonder, considering what hatred and rage they came withal. We were beholden to God, who tied their hands and saved our lives.

Newcastle spent a second night at Bolling Hall, where, as local legend has it, he was visited during the night by a spirit, which implored him to 'Pity poor Bradford'. His intention may have been to storm the town the next morning, with little quarter given to its defenders. There was little love lost between the Yorkshire Royalists and the inhabitants of Bradford, and an opportunity had arisen for them to wreak their revenge against the town. The Royalists had attempted to capture the town on 18 December 1642. During their repulse a Royalist officer, possibly the Earl of Newport's son, had asked for quarter and had been cut down by two local men, who were unaware that their unfortunate victim had been asking for mercy. The term 'Bradford quarter' arose from this incident, and indeed it was 'Bradford quarter' that the town expected to receive on 2 July. Had Newcastle ever issued an order to massacre the inhabitants? With his previous and subsequent record it seems unlikely. When the Royalist army marched into Bradford they captured 15 officers and 300 soldiers. Two hundred of their own men, who had previously been captured, possibly at Wakefield, were released. Three hours after his army occupied Bradford, Newcastle received more good news – the enemy had abandoned Leeds, and its remaining garrison and its armoury had been captured by Royalist prisoners, who then went on to release 700 more of their comrades. Once again these were probably men captured at Wakefield in May.

As Newcastle's forces were occupying Bradford, Sir Thomas Fairfax was arriving at Leeds, where he found a chaotic scene:

> I found all in great distraction here; the Council of War newly risen, where it was resolved to quit the town and make our retreat to Hull (which was 60 miles off, and many garrisons of the enemy in the way) which in 2

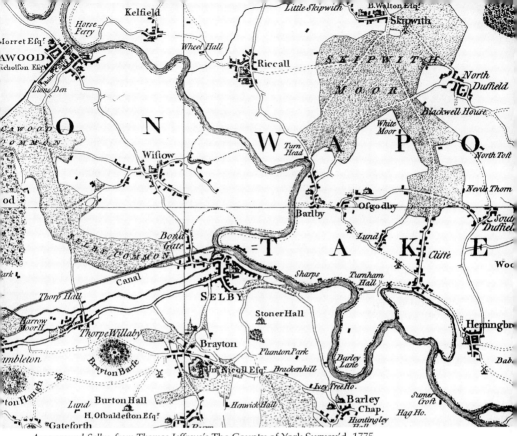

Area around Selby, from Thomas Jeffreys's The County of York Survey'd, *1775.*

hours time was done; for we could expect no less than that the enemy should presently send horse to prevent it, for they had 50 or 60 troops within 3 miles.

Sir Thomas must have been exhausted by the time he reached Leeds. He had arisen early on the morning of 30 June, fought the Battle of Adwalton Moor, withdrawn to Halifax and then marched to Bradford during the night, led the defence of the town on 1 July, and broken out and marched to Leeds during the night. Many of his father's men must have been in a similar state. Now, only two hours after arriving at Leeds, Sir Thomas was on the move again. The Fairfaxes' departure from Leeds must have been at between seven and eight in the morning. By far the most detailed account of the retreat to Hull is Sir Thomas's own, and this will be quoted at length. Moving along what is now the A63, the Fairfaxes made for Selby, and its crossing of the River Ouse, a major barrier between them and the safety of Hull. Close to Selby lay a substantial enemy garrison, at Cawood Castle, and a force of horse was despatched to intercept the Fairfaxes, catching up with them in Selby. Sir Thomas tells of his rearguard action to make time for his father, and the pitiful remnants of his army, to cross the Ouse:

Junction of Gowthorpe (straight ahead) and Brayton Lane (left).

But we got well to Selby, where there was a ferry, and hard by a garrison at Cawood. My Father being a mile before me with a few men, getting over the ferry, word came to us that he was in danger to be taken. I hasted to him with about 40 horse, the rest coming on after, in some disorder. He was newly got into the boat. The enemy with three cornets of horse entering the town, I was drawn up in the market place; they turned on the right hand, with part of my Troop I charged them in the flank and so divided them. We had the chase of them down the long street that did go to Brayton. It happened at the same time, those men that I had left behind were coming up the street, but (being in some disorder and under discouragements of the misfortunes of many days before) turned about, and gave way, not knowing that we were pursuing them in the rear. At the end of this street was a narrow lane that led to Cawood. The enemy strove to pass away there, but being strait caused a sudden stop, where we mingled one among another. Here I received a shot in the wrist of my arm which made the bridle fall out of my hand, which being among the nerves and veins, suddenly let out such a quantity of blood, that I was ready to fall from my horse; so taking the reins in the other hand, in which I had my sword, (the enemy minding nothing so much as how to get

Looking up Gowthorpe towards the Market Place and abbey. Part of the Royalist horse routed down this street.

The fog of war – musketeers fire a volley. Courtesy of John Wilson

away) I drew myself out of the crowd, and came to our men that turned about, which were standing hard by; seeing me ready to fall from my horse, they laid me on the ground, and now almost senseless. My surgeon came seasonably and bound up my wound, so stopped the bleeding. After a quarter of an hours rest, I got back on horseback again. The other part of our horse also beat the enemy to Cawood, back again that way they came first to us; so through the goodness of God, our passage here was made clear.

Three cornets of horse indicate that the Royalist horse was made up of three troops, or somewhere in the region of 150 men. Fairfax had deployed his forty men in the market place, and awaited his enemy's arrival. Approaching from Cawood the Royalist horse would have entered Selby along Millgate, and turned left into Micklegate. They would have continued into Finkle Street and then emerged into the Market Place, where Sir Thomas's men struck them in the flank, splitting them in two. One part of the Royalist force fled down Gowthorpe, and here they ran into more of Fairfax's men straggling into the town. Discouraged by the events of the past few days, the Parliamentary troopers turned and galloped away, not realising that the enemy thundering towards them were actually running away and were being pursued by part of Sir Thomas's force. The other half of the Royalist force fled back up Finkle Street and Micklegate, pursued by Sir Thomas and the remainder of his men, until they reached the entry into Millgate, which was so narrow that it formed a choke point, and brought them to a halt. During the fighting, as the Royalist horsemen tried to force their way out of Micklegate, Sir Thomas was wounded in the wrist by a pistol shot. Fortunately, the enemy seemed to be more intent on getting away than fighting, and Sir Thomas was able to withdraw and have his wound dressed. While this was happening the enemy was chased out of the town.

By the time Sir Thomas had had his wound dressed his father had crossed the

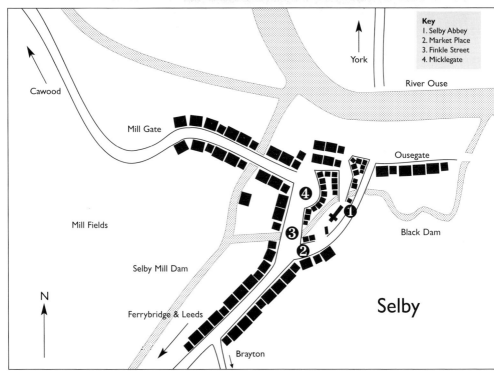

Key
1. Selby Abbey
2. Market Place
3. Finkle Street
4. Micklegate

York

River Ouse

Cawood

Mill Gate

Ousegate

Mill Fields

Black Dam

Selby Mill Dam

Selby

N

Ferrybridge & Leeds

Brayton

Ouse and was on his way to Hull. Sir Thomas continues the story:

So we went over the ferry after my Father. Myself, with others, went through the levels to Hull; but it proved a very troublesome and dangerous passage, having often interruptions from the enemy, sometimes on our front, sometimes in our rear. Now I had been at least 20 hours on horseback (after I was shot) without any rest or refreshment, and as many hours before: And as a further addition to my afflictions, my

Finkle Street looking towards Micklegate. Sir Thomas Fairfax pursued the Royalist horse down Finkle Street into Micklegate.

Looking along Micklegate towards Millgate. Sir Thomas Fairfax's Horse pursued the routing Royalist Horse along the street and Fairfax received a pistol wound in the wrist.

daughter (not above 5 years old, being carried before her Maid) endured all this retreat on horseback; but Nature not able to hold out longer, she fell into swoonings frequently, and happen ready to expire her last. And having now passed the Trent, and seeing a house not very far off, I sent her with her maid, thither, with little hopes of seeing her any more alive; but intending the next day, to send a ship from Hull for her; so I went to Barton (having sent before to have a ship ready against my coming thither). Here I laid down a little, to rest, if it were possible to find any in a body so full of pain, and a mind so full of anxiety and trouble. (Though I must confess it as the infinite goodness of God to me, though my spirits were nothing at all discouraged from doing still, that which I thought to be

Finkle Street looking towards the Market Place. The Royalist horse approached the Market Place down this street.

Market Place looking down Gowthorpe.

my work and duty) but I had not laid above a quarter of an hour, before the enemy came close to the town. I had, now, not above 100 horse with me. We went to the ship, where under the cover of her ordinance, we got all our men and horse aboard; so passing Humber, we arrived at Hull. Our men faint and tired; myself having lost all, even to my shirt (for my clothes were made unfit to wear with rends and blood which was upon them).

Sir Thomas must be mistaken when he says he crossed the Ouse at Selby, as a glance at a map of the East Riding will show. If he had done so, he would have been moving along the north bank of the Humber, not the south bank, crossing the Trent and marching to Barton in Lincolnshire.

The Fairfaxes, with the remnants of their army, were now penned up in Hull. The Duchess of Newcastle sums up the results of the Battle of Adwalton Moor:

By which victory the enemy was so daunted, that they forsook the rest of their garrisons, that is to say, Halifax, Leeds, and Wakefield, and dispersed themselves severally, the chief officers retiring to Hull, a strong garrison of the enemy; and though my Lord, knowing they would make their escape thither, as having no other place of refuge to resort to, sent a letter to York to the Governor of that city, to stop them in their passage; yet by neglect of the post, it coming not timely enough into his hands, his design was frustrated.

The whole county of York, save only Hull, being now cleared and settled by my Lord's care and conduct, he marched into the city of York, and having a competent number of horse well armed and commanded, he quartered them in the East Riding, near Hull, there being no visible enemy then to oppose them.

With the Fairfaxes' retreat to Hull, Newcastle gained control of the rest of the county. While Newcastle had reached the peak of his success, the Fairfaxes' fortunes had hit rock bottom. It would remain to be seen what Newcastle would do with the opportunity he was presented.

CHAPTER IX

Parliament resurgent
– the storming of Selby

The enemy within defended themselves stoutly, a good while. Sir Thomas Fairfax

The immediate effect of the battle of Adwalton Moor was to place the whole of Yorkshire, with the exception of Hull, within Newcastle's control. He was now presented with an opportunity to make a major contribution to the Royalist war effort by marching south and reinforcing the King. In conjunction with other events elsewhere in the country, this could have proved a war-winning strategy.

Once again it was the Yorkshire gentry who thwarted Newcastle's plans, as they were loath to leave the county while Lord Fairfax held firm in Hull, even though Newcastle had quartered a large body of horse close to the town to prevent Parliamentary incursions. Newcastle had moved part of his army into Lincolnshire and had recaptured Lincoln and Gainsborough, and was ready to march south. Unfortunately, towards the end of August he began to receive a number of complaints from the East Riding gentry that Sir Thomas Fairfax was raiding far and wide, and had even reached Stamford Bridge to the east of York. Leaving part of his army in Lincolnshire, Newcastle returned to Yorkshire, and, having decided to finish off the troublesome Fairfaxes once and for all, laid siege to Hull on 2 September.

While Newcastle prevaricated, Parliament had set in motion a train of events that would have a major effect on the subsequent course of the war. On the evening after Adwalton Moor, Thomas Stockdale, a close associate of Lord Fairfax, had written a letter from Halifax to the speaker of the House of Commons, William Lenthall, outlining the day's course of events, and the magnitude of Lord Fairfax's defeat. This letter was read to both Houses on 5 July, and galvanised Parliament to go down a road they had been considering for some time – alliance with the Scots. Although subsequent events reinforced this decision, the trigger to send representatives to Scotland was Newcastle's victory at Adwalton Moor. On 25 September Parliament ratified an agreement with the

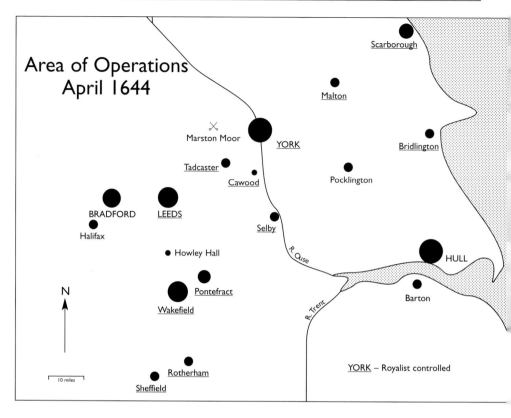

Area of Operations
April 1644

Scarborough

Malton

Marston Moor

YORK

Bridlington

Tadcaster

Cawood

Pocklington

BRADFORD

LEEDS

Halifax

Selby

Howley Hall

R. Ouse

HULL

N

Pontefract

Barton

Wakefield

R. Trent

10 miles

Rotherham

Sheffield

YORK – Royalist controlled

Scots – the Solemn League and Covenant. Although this agreement contained political and religious clauses, the most important part of it, as far as the Civil War in Yorkshire is concerned, was the proposed invasion of northern England by a Scottish army of 20,000 men. Due to wrangling between the Scots and Parliament, the military aspects of the agreement were not completed until November 1643, which meant that the Scottish army was not ready to march until January 1644.

Back in Yorkshire, the siege of Hull progressed slowly, with the Royalist besiegers literally getting bogged down when Lord Fairfax opened the River Hull's floodgates and inundated the land around the town. Fairfax was reinforced in early October by Sir John Meldrum, whose previous time in Hull had prevented the town being handed to the King by Sir John Hotham, in the lead up to hostilities. With the start of the siege, Sir Thomas Fairfax and a large contingent of his father's horse had been transferred by boat into Lincolnshire, where he joined with the Earl of Manchester's Eastern Association Lieutenant-General of Horse, one Oliver Cromwell.

Oliver Cromwell (1599-1658)

Oliver Cromwell was born into a middling yeoman family in Huntingdonshire on 25 April 1599. He began his education at Sydney Sussex College, Cambridge, but returned home to Huntingdon after his father's death in June 1617. On 22 August 1620 he married Elizabeth Bourchier, who bore him eight children: four sons and four daughters. In March 1628 Cromwell entered Parliament as the Member for Huntingdon, and served until King Charles dissolved Parliament in 1629, when he returned to his estate.

In 1640 Cromwell returned to Parliament as the Member for Cambridge. With the outbreak of the 1st Civil War he raised a troop of horse, which was incorporated into the Earl of Essex's army. There is some dispute about whether or not he took part in the Battle of Edgehill, and it is likely that his troop did not arrive on the battlefield until very late in the day, after the fighting had ceased.

Returning to East Anglia, Cromwell was promoted to colonel in the army of the Eastern Association, where he busied himself recruiting and training a large regiment of horse, soon to become known as the Ironsides. The campaigning in Lincolnshire saw Cromwell's reputation as a competent, sometimes brilliant, cavalry commander established, and it was here that he first fought alongside Sir Thomas Fairfax, when their combined forces defeated a large Royalist force at Winceby in October 1643.

The summer of 1644 saw the army of the Eastern Association, combined with Lord Fairfax and the Scots army, besieging York, and Cromwell was instrumental in the defeat of the Royalists at Marston Moor. In the aftermath of the fall of York, the army of the Eastern Association moved south to combine with Parliamentary forces and fight the King's army at the inconclusive battle of Newbury on 27 October. Some members of Parliament, Cromwell included, were not impressed with the performance of Parliament's senior commanders, and in December 1644 the Self Denying Ordinance was signed, which prevented members of either house from commanding troops, although Cromwell avoided having to resign his commission.

In early 1645 Parliament formed its New Model Army, which Sir Thomas Fairfax was appointed to command, with Cromwell as his lieutenant-general. This proved to be a war-winning team, and after the defeat of the King's army at Naseby on 14 June 1645, Charles's cause was lost, although the war continued for almost a year. Cromwell was one of the regicides who called for the King's execution, after the King had refused to come to terms with Parliament. After the King's execution in January 1649, Cromwell campaigned in Ireland, where he gained a reputation for brutality at such places as Drogheda and Wexford. In 1650 the 3rd Civil War erupted, and Cromwell led the New Model Army to victory over the Scots at Dunbar on 3 September 1650.

His greatest victory, at Worcester, came on the same date in 1651.

In 1653 Cromwell dissolved the Rump of the Long Parliament, and, after two abortive Protectorate parliaments, he was declared Lord Protector in 1657, a position he continued to hold until his death on 3 September 1658. Cromwell is quite often considered to be a dour Puritan, but as a young man, prior to his marriage, he had a reputation for being 'more famous at football, cudgels, or any other boisterous sport or game than at his books', and throughout his life he enjoyed a joke, and music and dancing.

On 11 October, Newcastle received two hammer blows. The first was the defeat of his army in Lincolnshire at the battle of Winceby, where Sir Thomas Fairfax and Oliver Cromwell combined to rout a sizeable Royalist force, although Cromwell was unhorsed and in danger of his life for a short time. The second was a major sally by the garrison of Hull, which, pushing along the bank of the Humber, drove the besiegers back in disarray for several miles, and captured a number of large Royalist artillery pieces. On 12 October the Royalists raised the siege and withdrew towards York, and with this withdrawal active campaigning in Yorkshire seems to have come to an end. Lord Fairfax gathered his strength in Hull, while his son was campaigning in Lincolnshire and Derbyshire. Newcastle, recently promoted in the peerage to Marquess, seems to have gone into winter quarters at his house at Welbeck quite early. All three awaited events in the north.

On the morning of 19 January 1644 the Scottish army, in three separate columns, invaded Northumbria. There were twenty-one regiments of foot, seven regiments of horse, and approximately 18,000 men, complete with a large train of artillery. Sir Thomas Glemham had been despatched to Northumbria to hold the Scots, but his pitifully small force, less than 2,000 men, could do little to oppose the massive Scottish army, other than break down bridges and try to obstruct the roads south. The Scottish commander, Alexander Leslie, Earl of Leven, a canny old soldier, paused for several days to allow his columns to close up, before continuing his march towards Newcastle-upon-Tyne, reaching Alnwick on 25 January and Morpeth on the 27th. The weather now took a turn for the worse, and the Scots remained quartered around Morpeth until 1 February, when the march towards Newcastle recommenced, although the weather worsened on the 2nd, preventing the Scots from reaching the town until the 3rd. This day's delay made all the difference, as the Marquess of Newcastle threw his army into the town whose name he bore only hours before the Scots arrived.

Newcastle had returned to York on, or about, 15 January, having been promised 10,000 new recruits by the Yorkshire gentry, few of whom were forthcoming. News reached him at York that the Scots were massing along the border, in preparation for their long-expected invasion. Newcastle's intention had been to leave Sir William Saville, who had been governor of York and commanded the troops in Yorkshire while Newcastle was in Lincolnshire and in winter quarters, in command in the county while he marched north to oppose the Scots. Unfortunately, Saville passed away prior to Newcastle's march north, and Colonel

John Belasyse had been ordered north from the King's Oxford army to replace him. Belasyse was an experienced soldier who had marched south with the King in August 1643.

On 29 January Newcastle began his march north, with 5,000 infantry and 3,000 cavalry. James King, Newcastle's Lieutenant-General, newly raised to the peerage as Lord Eythin, preceded the army and arrived at Newcastle to find the town still well disposed to the King's cause, and actively preparing for the arrival of the Scots. Newcastle followed on with the main force and arrived at the town a few hours before the Scots, having marched from York to Newcastle in only five days.

The Scots summoned the town and, expecting little resistance, were surprised to get a reply from the Marquess of Newcastle, whom they still believed to be much further south. Newcastle was a tough nut to crack, as it could only be attacked from three sides, the fourth being protected by the Tyne. Reinforcements and supplies could be moved into the town at will while the Royalists controlled the south bank of the river. The defence of the Tyne became Newcastle's main priority, and the bulk of his army was deployed to defend the crossing points to the west of the town, with the Scots moving further and further west in the hope of finding an undefended ford. On 19 February Newcastle realised that the Scots were spread very thinly along the north bank of the Tyne, and decided to strike at the western end of the line. A plan was hatched to attack a Scots quarter holding several regiments of horse, at Corbridge. Sir Marmaduke Langdale, a dour Yorkshireman, as he is often described, would lead a column of horse and musketeers to attack the Scots from the west, while another column, commanded by Colonel Brandling, attacked from the east. In a hard-fought action the Scottish horse were defeated, and the Scots withdrew their troops into a much smaller area closer to Newcastle.

The Scots were in a poor situation. It was midwinter, and their supply lines stretched back to Scotland, along little more than dirt tracks, and no decent port existed between Newcastle and Berwick. A decision was taken to force the Tyne, and to march on Sunderland, a good port, which would provide them with a firm supply base. At the same time the Marquess of Newcastle had decided that his army needed to rest, as the constant patrolling and skirmishing, in winter weather, were wearing both his men and horses out. He also realised that there were too many crossing points for him to defend them all in strength, so he took a decision to let the Scots cross: 'So I resolved of two evils to choose the less, and left them to their own wills'.

The Scots finally crossed the Tyne on 28 February, using three separate fords, and continued their marches for the next few days, until they arrived at Sunderland and occupied it on 4 March. Several Scots writers express surprise at the lack of opposition on their march, and Leven expected the Royalists to hold the line of the River Wear, a few miles from Sunderland. For the next four weeks the Scots remained close to Sunderland, gathering supplies and preparing for the march south.

Newcastle tried to draw the Scots into the open field, where his superior horse would provide him with an important advantage. Leven, experienced soldier that he was, refused to be drawn, and a number of indecisive engagements were fought in the enclosures to the west and north of Sunderland, with Leven using the terrain to his advantage by negating the Royalist superiority in mounted troops. On 25 March, Newcastle realised that Leven would not be drawn out to fight him in the open, and took the decision to fall back to his quarters around Durham. On 31 March the Scots followed him, arriving at Quarrington Hill, a few miles east of Durham, on 8 April, effectively cutting Newcastle off from Hartlepool, his main supply port in the area.

On 12 April Newcastle received grievous news from Yorkshire – Selby had fallen, and with it a large part of his remaining forces in the county. He took decisive action, and in the early hours of the 13th began a rapid march back to York, hoping to arrive there before the Parliamentarians occupied it. The Scots pursued him closely, capturing many stragglers. Newcastle reached York on the 19th, and the Scottish and Parliamentary armies rendezvoused at Tadcaster on the following day. The situation in the north had changed dramatically over a period of only a few weeks.

When Newcastle marched north on 29 January, he had left Colonel John Belasyse with a force of 3,000 foot and 1,500 horse, scattered in garrisons throughout the county. Belasyse began to raise recruits, both for his own force and to send to the Earl of Newcastle in the north.

By the end of February pressure had begun to grow on the Royalists in Yorkshire. From Hull, Lord Fairfax's men were growing more daring, as opposition to them lessened. In early February Lord Fairfax had ordered Sir William Constable to carry out a mounted raid in the East Riding, which reached as far north as Pickering. Belasyse despatched a large force of cavalry to intercept Constable, but they were unable to locate him. Constable did not have the same problem, and surprised three regiments of Royalist horse in their quarters, capturing a large number of prisoners, before returning to Hull.

In Nottinghamshire, a large force of Parliamentary troops, under the ubiquitous Sir John Meldrum, laid siege to Newark, and this force threatened South Yorkshire. At the same time Colonel John Lambert led a small force from Lancashire to occupy Bradford, and this was the vanguard of Sir Thomas Fairfax's returning troops. After operating in Lincolnshire, Sir Thomas and his men had been despatched by Parliament into Cheshire to relieve Nantwich, which was besieged by Sir John Byron's Royalist army. Recruiting troops in Lancashire as he went, Fairfax arrived at Nantwich on 25 January, decisively beating the besiegers and relieving the town. Returning to Lancashire he continued to recruit and train men in preparation for his return to his home county. Lambert was the vanguard of this return.

Accompanying Lambert was Captain John Hodgson, a participant at the defence of Bradford in December 1642 and the battle of Seacroft Moor. He writes of their return to the town, sometime in late February or early March 1644:

> We found the enemy in Bradford, but they over-run the church. Our horse had some bickering with them up to the lane head, and was put to flight; but our foot gave them such a salute with shot, as made them run for it.

Although the date of Lambert's occupation of Bradford is not known, what is clear is that he was in the town by 6 March, as he wrote a letter from there to Sir Thomas

Fairfax, outlining a raid on an enemy quarter at Hunslet, where a large number of prisoners were taken.

In response to the Parliamentary incursions in the East and West Ridings, and the threat from Nottinghamshire, Belasyse began a reorganisation of his forces, which he divided into three main bodies, one at Leeds to cover the West Riding, one at Malton to cover the East Riding, and a third at York to cover the North Riding and act in support of the other two. Further to this, garrisons of foot were placed in Halifax, Doncaster, and Stamford Bridge. At the same time Belasyse had gathered a force of around 1,500 horse and 5,000 foot at Selby, which he made his headquarters. Belasyse had been ordered to adopt a defensive stance by Newcastle, and his deployment makes sense in this light.

On 5 March the Committee of Both Kingdoms, a committee made up of both English and Scottish representatives, and tasked with the day-to-day running of the war, sent similar orders to Lord Fairfax and his son:

> The Committee of Both Kingdoms to Ferdinando Lord Fairfax. We have considered the opportunity that is now offered for reducing and assuring of Yorkshire whilst the Marquis of Newcastle has drawn the greatest part of his forces towards the north to oppose the Scots, and how necessary it is to hinder all further levies there to increase his army, which the better to effect, we have written to Sir Thomas Fairfax to forthwith march into the West Riding, with all his horse, and take with him two regiments of foot out of Lancashire. We desire that you will also take the field with as great a force of horse and foot as you can, and joining with Sir Thomas Fairfax make the best advantage you can of the present opportunity and of those forces for effecting the ends aforesaid. We also desire that you will hold a continual intelligence with the Scottish army, and by drawing near to the Tees or otherwise to give them the best accommodation you shall be able, and that you will continually advertise us all your occurrences and affairs.

With this order from Parliament, events began to move rapidly. On 21 March Prince Rupert, the King's nephew, surprised Sir John Meldrum's besieging army at Newark, and forced it to surrender. This freed up a force of 1,000 Nottinghamshire horse, under Sir Gervase Lucas and Colonel George Porter, to march into Yorkshire, and join with Belasyse, who had 1,000 foot and 500 horse, in an attack on Bradford, on or about 25 March. Lambert drew his horse out of the town and attacked the approaching enemy, but was driven back by sheer weight of numbers. The Royalist foot then assaulted the town, but were driven back by its garrison. This left the defenders low on powder, and at a council of war it was decided to break out towards Halifax. The breakout was successful, with Lambert's troopers breaking through George Porter's men and carrying on to Halifax. The Royalists occupied the town, but were also short of powder, so they decided to withdraw to Leeds. By nightfall both sides were withdrawing and leaving Bradford to its own devices, although Lambert quickly realised what was happening and reoccupied the town. Belasyse seems to have laid the blame for Lambert's escape on George Porter, and Porter took exception to this, returning to Newark with his men.

Prince Rupert (1619-1682)

Rupert was the second son of King Charles's sister Elizabeth, and was born in Prague on 17 December 1619. He began his military campaigning at an early age, during the Thirty Years War, and was captured during the battle of Vlotho on 17 October 1648. Rupert spent his time as a prisoner well, studying military manuals, shooting and playing tennis. He was released in late 1641, having promised not to fight against the emperor again, and even having been offered command of an Imperial Army, which he declined.

Events in England now took a hand; and Rupert crossed the Channel to join his uncle in February 1642, but returned to Holland with the Queen almost immediately. Remaining at his mother's court in the Hague until the summer of 1642, Rupert and his brother Maurice sailed to Tynemouth, and continued to Nottingham in time to join their uncle when he raised his royal standard on 22 August.

Rupert was appointed commander of the King's horse, and almost immediately came into conflict with other senior Royalist commanders. He very quickly began to build a reputation as an invincible commander, first beating a large force of Parliamentary horse at Powick Bridge on 23 September, and then driving the bulk of the enemy horse from the field at Edgehill on 23 October. The indiscipline of the Royalist horse, galloping in pursuit of the fleeing enemy, almost led to a Royalist defeat. After Edgehill Rupert put forward a plan for a rapid march on London, the Royalists having got between the Earl of Essex and the capital. The King chose a slower approach, which allowed Essex to return to London and confront him with a large, well positioned force at Turnham Green. Unable to regain his capital the King withdrew into winter quarters around Reading.

The early part of 1643 was taken up with raid and counter-raid, but in July Rupert was despatched to capture Bristol, which he stormed on 26 July. The Royalists' next target was Gloucester, the only remaining Parliamentary garrison in the Severn Valley, and the town was besieged in August. Essex marched from London and relieved the town, before setting off on his return march. The King's army set off in pursuit, and Rupert's dashing tactics managed to slow Essex's army down enough for the Royalists to get between them and London, at Newbury. In a hard-fought, drawn battle on 19 and 20 September the Parliamentary forces were brought to a halt, but the King's army had to withdraw due to a lack of powder.

In 1644 Rupert was at his most active, first relieving Newark in March, and then marching through Lancashire to relieve York, gathering his forces as he went and capturing Bolton and Liverpool. He successfully relieved York on

1 July, but was badly defeated at Marston Moor on the following day, his first defeat.

In 1645 the Royalist cause took a turn for the worse, when the King's army was defeated at Naseby on 14 June. Rupert's horse, on the Royalist right wing, had swept their opponents from the field, but had then galloped off in pursuit, not returning to the field until after the remainder of their army had been soundly defeated. After Naseby, Rupert was given the command of the garrison at Bristol, a vital port and arms manufactory. With no prospect of relief Rupert surrendered the town to Sir Thomas Fairfax on 10 September 1645, against his uncle's express orders. He was banished from the King's presence and left for the Continent, never to return during his uncle's lifetime. In later life Rupert turned from land warfare and became an Admiral, commanding a fleet against Parliament in 1648, and against the Dutch after the Restoration of Charles II.

Rupert was a blunt soldier, which caused problems with his uncle's courtiers. He was a very effective cavalry commander, and rarely defeated, although his headlong charges could lead to problems as his men set off in pursuit of the enemy, leaving the remainder of the army to fend for itself. He also introduced several Continental methods of siege warfare, including mining. His defeat at Marston Moor seems to have affected him badly, and he carried his uncle's letter, which he believed was a direct order to fight, with him until his dying day.

On 1 April the Committee of Both Kingdoms despatched orders to the two Fairfaxes, ordering them to combine their forces and march north to the aid of the Scots. By the time these orders had arrived the Fairfaxes had put another plan into action, and the whole situation in the north had changed – they would attack Belasyse's main force at Selby. On 9 April Lord Fairfax and his son met at Ferrybridge, and on 10 April their combined force began its approach march.

In a letter to the Committee of Both Kingdoms, Lord Fairfax gave the strength of his army at Selby as 2,000 foot and 2,000 horse and dragoons, while he reported Belasyse as having 1,500 horse and 1,800 foot. These figures may be a little high, as his son gives the Royalists a combined strength of only 2,000 men, although the number of prisoners taken suggests that the numbers are not too greatly exaggerated. The rest of Belasyse's forces had been dispersed in garrisons. As the Parliamentary forces approached, Belasyse despatched a body of horse to intercept them, but this was rapidly driven back into the town by Fairfax's mounted advance guard, losing a number of prisoners in the fight. By nightfall the Parliamentary army had closed up on Selby, and Fairfax sent a summons for the town to surrender, which Belasyse promptly refused, and both armies hunkered down for the night and prepared for the morrow's fight.

Although Selby was not a fortified town, nature had made it a difficult place to attack, as it was almost surrounded by water obstacles. Along its north side ran the

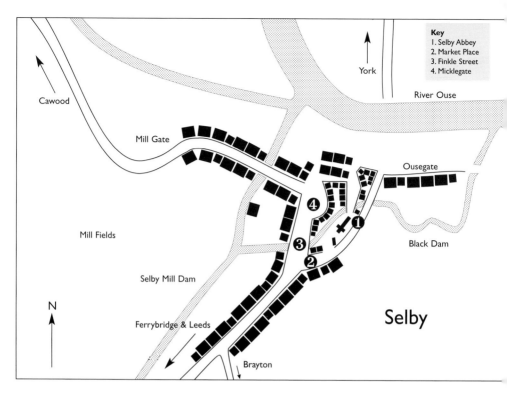

Key
1. Selby Abbey
2. Market Place
3. Finkle Street
4. Micklegate

York

River Ouse

Cawood

Mill Gate

Ousegate

Mill Fields

Black Dam

Selby Mill Dam

N

Selby

Ferrybridge & Leeds

Brayton

Ouse, and to the west ran the Selby Mill Dam, which flowed into the river. To the east were the old fishponds of the abbey, and these ponds and the Mill Dam had a tendency to flood during wet periods, and this does seem to have been the case in April 1644. The only access to the town not covered by water was from the south, between Gowthorpe and Brayton Lane, but Lord Fairfax had remedied this during his occupation of the town after the battle of Tadcaster, when he dug a ditch between the two lanes. Four roads entered the town, and, because of the water obstacles, these would prove to be the only access points. To the east Ousegate ran alongside the river, as its name suggests, and was the widest street in the town, which also made it the hardest to defend. Gowthorpe and Brayton Lane entered the town from the south, with Brayton Lane joining Gowthorpe several hundred yards from the Market Place, the centre of the town. Finally, there was Mill Lane, which was so narrow that the defenders had not even barricaded it, a decision that was borne out when Lord Fairfax chose not to attack it.

Fairfax planned to hit the town from three directions simultaneously, along Ousegate, Gowthorpe and Brayton Lane, and with this in mind he divided his force into three bodies, each containing horse and foot. The foot would assault the barricades and clear an entrance for the horse, which would then attack towards the Market Place. Lord Fairfax commanded the troops attacking along Ousegate, while his son commanded their supporting horse. The other two bodies were commanded by Sir John Meldrum, exchanged after his capture at Newark, and Colonel Needham, although it is unclear which body attacked Gowthorpe, and which attacked Brayton Lane.

Most of the contemporary accounts of the storming are very much in agreement. In his report to the Committee of Both Kingdoms, Lord Fairfax wrote:

> The enemy received us with much courage, and made strong resistance for two hours or thereabouts; but in conclusion, my own foot regiment forced a passage by the river side, and my son with his regiment of horse rushed into the town, where he encountered Colonel Belasyse, and the enemy's horse; but they being beaten back, and Master Belasyse himself wounded and taken prisoner, and our foot entered the town on all sides of the town, the enemy was wholly routed, and as many as could saved themselves by flight, some towards Cawood [along Mill Lane], some towards Pontefract, and the rest towards York, over the river by a bridge of boats laid by themselves. We pursued them every way, and took in the town and chase, the prisoners, ordnance, arm ammunition, and colours mentioned in the list enclosed [discussed below].

Lord Fairfax succinctly sums up the course of the fight, and his son's account follows similar lines:

> The enemy within defended themselves stoutly, a good while; our men, at length, beat them from the line, but could not advance further, because of the horse within. I getting a barricade open, which let us in between the

Ousegate. Parliamentary troops broke into the town along this street. Sir Thomas Fairfax's horse charged along the street towards the camera.

Ousegate. Looking towards Royalist barricade.

houses and the river, we had an encounter with their horse. After one charge they fled over a bridge of boats to York. Other horse came up and charged us again, where my horse was overthrown, being single, a little before my men, who presently relieved me, and forced the enemy back, who retreated also to York. In this charge we took Colonel Belasyse, governor of York. By this time the foot had entered the town, and also took many prisoners.

Here is a repeat of Sir Thomas's exploit at Wakefield, separated from his men in the midst of the enemy. Belasyse's secretary, Joshua Moone, who wrote a brief biography of Belasyse entitled *A Brief Relation of the Life and Memoirs of John Lord Belasyse*, supports Sir Thomas's account:

By break of day he defended the place gallantly for the space of eight or ten hours, and at the last by the treachery or cowardice of one Captain Williams, afterwards condemned to death by a council of war, at his post, Sir Thomas Fairfax's horse entered; whereupon my Lord charged him in person at the head of his horse. But they (the officers only excepted) not advancing, but taking occasion to fly over the aforesaid bridge of boats, he found himself engaged in the midst of Sir Thomas Fairfax's troops, who killed his horse under him and discharged some pistols and blows with swords at him; so as he had certainly been slain but for the goodness of his arms, and thereby received but two wounds; one in his arm, the other in his head; both with swords: so as (though he asked it not), yet they gave him quarter, and carried him to the Lord Fairfax, their General and my Lord's near kinsman, who treated him civilly and sent his surgeon to dress his wounds, and ordered his going down the river, together with Sir John Ramsden, Sir Thomas Strickland and other prisoners to Hull.

The fighting seems to have lasted for a long time, although Moone's 'eight or ten hours' may be an exaggeration. Lord Fairfax's men eventually cleared the Royalist defenders from the barricade at the end of Ousegate, but could not enter the street because of the Royalist horse. Sir Thomas Fairfax and his men managed to clear the barricade and enter the town; Moone puts this down to the treachery or cowardice of a Royalist officer, and a charge of the enemy horse that promptly broke the defence. Belasyse led a counter-attack with fresh horse, during which Sir Thomas was unhorsed and separated from his men. The Parliamentary horse then renewed its attack, relieving Sir Thomas, and it was then Belasyse's turn to be unhorsed, and subsequently

Ousegate looking back towards the abbey. Parliamentary Horse charged down the street towards the Market Place.

Musketeers on sentry duty. Courtesy of John Wilson

wounded and captured.

With his loss the heart went out of the Royalist defenders, and the attackers were able to enter at all three points. Those defenders who could escaped from the town, mainly the horse, and the remainder fell captive with their commander. Lord Fairfax reported the capture of eighty named officers, 1,600 common soldiers, a large quantity of arms and ammunition: four brass cannon, 2,000 arms, seven barrels of powder and sixteen bundles of match, and these captured supplies would have been a great boon to Fairfax.

With the fall of Selby the situation in Yorkshire and the north east changed dramatically. Newcastle raced south upon receiving the news, hotly pursued by the Scots. On 20 April the Scots army and Lord Fairfax's joined at Tadcaster, and this allied army then marched on York, arriving before its walls on the 22nd. During the night Newcastle despatched his horse from York towards the south, having decided to stand a siege, during which his horse would be extra mouths to feed, and fodder would have to be found for their mounts. Realising Newcastle's cavalry, henceforth referred to as the Northern Horse, had escaped from the city, the Allied cavalry set off in pursuit, killing and capturing a small number before the Royalists managed to escape. On 23 April the Allied army began to dig its siege lines, and the siege of York began.

CHAPTER X

The great and close siege of York
– the attack on the King's Manor

Being ambitious to have the honour, alone, of springing the mine. Sir Thomas Fairfax

The Allies moved into their positions around York, with Lord Fairfax's army, reinforced by several regiments of Scottish foot, covering the area to the east of the town, between the Ouse and the Foss, and the Scots deployed on the south and west sides of the town. Although they vastly outnumbered the Royalists, they did not have enough men to completely encircle the town, and the area between the Ouse and the Foss to the north was only covered by scattered cavalry patrols. This was a far from satisfactory situation.

On 5 May the Earl of Manchester's Eastern Association army captured Lincoln, which opened up the way to the north. The Earl of Crawford-Lindsay, a Scottish officer and nobleman, and Sir Thomas Fairfax met with the Earl of Manchester to urge him to move his army to York, which would give the Allies enough troops to completely surround the town, and Manchester readily agreed to this. On 24 May, after sending some of his troops to prepare the way, Manchester's army set off from Lincoln. After an uneventful march they arrived at Selby on the 28th. Over the next three days meetings were held to decide upon a course of action, and how Manchester's forces would fit into the siege lines. Once this was decided the Eastern Association troops began their march to York on 1 June.

On the same day the Earl of Manchester wrote to the Committee of Both Kingdoms to inform them that Sir John Meldrum had been despatched from York to the town of Manchester, with two regiments of foot, one of them Scots, to oppose Prince Rupert's march through Lancashire, which will be discussed further in due course. This letter was also the first indication to Parliament that the triumvirate of generals, Fairfax, Leven and Manchester, was determined to carry the siege of York to its conclusion, and not divide their forces, or raise the siege to react to Rupert's movements. This would become a continuing theme in the correspondence between the three generals and the Committee.

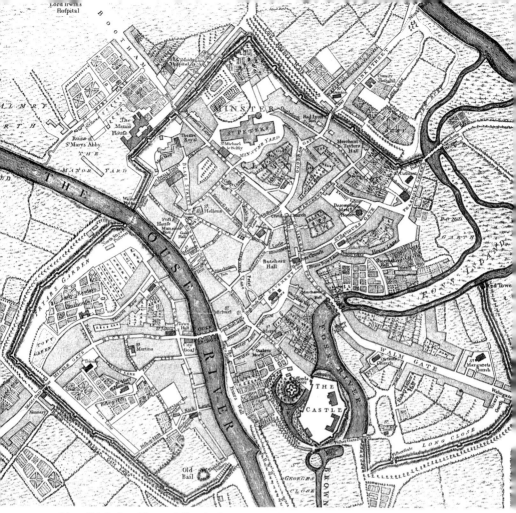

Map of York, from Thomas Jeffreys's The County of York Survey'd, *1775.*

On 3 June Manchester's army completed its march, and filed into its siege positions on the north-west side of York. Most of the horse of all three armies were despatched into the West Riding, where they would cover the passes between Yorkshire and Lancashire, and prevent Prince Rupert from crossing the Pennines in an attempt to raise the siege. With the arrival of Manchester's army, York was fully encircled, and a formal siege of the town, the largest of the Civil Wars, could begin.

After a long march on 3 June, it would be expected that Manchester's men would have rested on the 4th, but this does not seem to have been the case, and Simeon Ashe, the Earl of Manchester's chaplain, writes that 'some of them upon their own accord went up to the walls of York, and fetched out of the pastures there oxen, kine [cattle] and some horse'. These raids and counter-raids continued for several days.

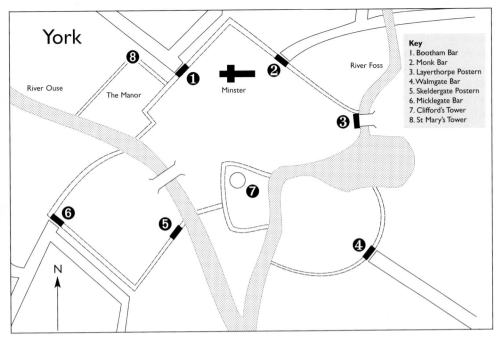

York

Key
1. Bootham Bar
2. Monk Bar
3. Layerthorpe Postern
4. Walmgate Bar
5. Skeldergate Postern
6. Micklegate Bar
7. Clifford's Tower
8. St Mary's Tower

River Foss

River Ouse

The Manor

Minster

N

On 5 June the Allies put into action a plan to raise a battery against Walmgate Bar, on the east side of York. The Scottish and Eastern Association armies formed up and advanced towards the walls, as though they were about to assault the town, but this was only a decoy. While the defenders' attention was drawn to the north and west sides of the town, Lord Fairfax captured the suburbs outside Walmgate Bar, and raised a battery of five guns within a couple of hundred yards of the gate. He deployed two further guns to cover the street, and a third gun close to a dovecote, which must have been a significant landmark at the time of the battle. Newcastle's failure to burn or demolish the suburbs outside the walls was a major error. Leaving the suburbs standing allowed his enemies a covered approach to the gates of the town, and defensible positions should the Royalists sally out. Learning from his mistake, Newcastle attempted, unsuccessfully, to fire the houses outside Bootham Bar, as Simeon Ashe reports:

Bootham Bar – looking up Bootham.

The wall of King's Manor showing chimneys for houses.

Upon Saturday the 8 day in the morning, a soldier of the Marquess of Newcastle was taken in the Earl of Manchester's leaguer: he was in a red suit, he had pitch, flax, and other materials upon him for the firing of the suburbs there, as yet free from the wasting flames. Some more of the Marquess's soldiers were taken prisoners also; they had white coats (made of plundered cloth taken from clothiers in these parts) with crosses on the sleeves, wrought with red and blue silk, an ensign as we conceive of some Popish regiment.

St Mary's Tower showing damage to the tower and adjacent wall.

Ashe also reports an attempt by Manchester's men to burn the wooden gate at Bootham Bar, but this too was unsuccessful, as the defenders threw grenades, ceramic spheres filled with gunpowder, from the walls.

Having received a communication from the Committee of Both Kingdoms, warning them of Prince Rupert's progress in Lancashire, the Allied commanders replied with a letter summing up their situation, and laying down their reasons for continuing the siege:

> For by this accession of forces Prince Rupert's army is so increased as we think it not safe to divide our men, and send a part to encounter him in Lancashire. If we should raise our siege before York and march with all our forces against him, it is in his discretion to avoid us, and either pass by another way than we take, and so come into Yorkshire, or else retire into Cheshire, whither if we should pursue him, it would be in the Marquis of Newcastle's power, in our absence, to recover all Yorkshire again and increase his army to as great a strength as ever it was.

It is much to their credit that the Allied commanders would not be stampeded into making a rash decision to split their force, or to raise the siege and cross the Pennines with their whole army. At this stage in the war, Prince Rupert had built up an aura of invincibility, with his rapid, decisive marches, as at Newark earlier in the year. Although his army in Lancashire was little more than half the strength of the Allied force at York, his reputation added greatly to its perceived strength, and gave his opponents pause.

In another letter to the Committee, the Earl of Manchester reported 'We are on all sides very near the town walls, and I hope within a few hours Sir James Lumsden and myself will have our mines ready, if not hindered by the tempestuous rainy weather'. Sir James Lumsden commanded the Scots foot sent to reinforce Lord Fairfax's army, and his men were engaged in digging a mine under Walmgate Bar, while Manchester's men were digging a second mine under St Mary's Tower, at the northernmost corner of the King's Manor, on the opposite side

Bowling Green – looking towards St Mary's Tower. It was in this area that the fighting took place.

of the town. Mines were simple tunnels under the section of the defences they were intended to destroy, with a chamber at the far end which would be packed with gunpowder, and the subsequent explosion could produce a significant breach. Storming parties would immediately attack the breach, while the defenders were still stunned and slow to react. At York the Allied commanders planned to explode two mines simultaneously on opposite sides of the town, not only attacking while the defenders were stunned, but forcing them to defend two breaches at the same time. Once again Newcastle's failure to burn the suburbs had come back to haunt him, as the mines were started within the cover of the suburbs, and thus had a much shorter distance to travel to reach the walls.

Newcastle had received news of Prince Rupert's advance, by fire signals from Pontefract Castle, which could be seen at night from York Minster's tower. Any time he could gain would aid Rupert's attempt to relieve him. With this in mind he sent two identical letters to Leven and Fairfax on the evening of 8 June:

> I cannot but admire that your Lordship hath so near beleaguered the city on all sides, made batteries against it, and so near approached it, without signifying what your intentions are, and what you desire or expect, which is contrary to the rules of all military discipline and customs; therefore I have thought fit to remonstrate thus much to your Lordship, to the end that your Lordship may signify your intentions and resolutions therein, and receive ours.

After over two weeks of siege Newcastle was asking the Allied commanders what their intentions were, and chiding them for not following the disciplines of war! What is even more incredible is that they fell for it, Leven replying on the same day:

> At this distance I will not dispute in points of military discipline, nor the practice of Captains in such cases, yet give your Lordship satisfaction in that your letter desires from me, your Lordship may take notice, I have drawn my forces before this city with intention to reduce it to the obedience due to the King and Parliament, whereupon if your Lordship shall speedily confer me, it may save the effusion of much innocent blood, whereof I wish your Lordship to be no less sparing than I am.

Although Leven had cast down his gauntlet, and refused to discuss the niceties of the disciplines of war with Newcastle, he had begun an exchange of communications that would last for a week, and gain Newcastle, and Rupert, seven precious days. The culmination of this exchange was a parley held on 14 June. On the 15th an exchange of conditions for the surrender of York changed hands, to which Newcastle replied:

> I have perused the Conditions and demands your Lordship sent, but when I considered the many professions made to avoid the effusion of Christian blood, I did admire to see such propositions from your Lordships, conceiving this not the way to it, for I cannot suppose that your Lordships do imagine that persons of honour can possibly condescend to any of these propositions.

With this firm refusal, Newcastle brought to an end the discussions, having achieved his aim of wasting as much time as was possible. That night an exchange of signals took place between York and Pontefract Castle, and this was assumed by the Allies to be a warning to Newcastle of Prince Rupert's imminent approach.

On 16 June Sir Henry Vane, a representative of the Committee of Both Kingdoms with the Allied armies at York, wrote a letter to the Committee outlining the completion of the two mines and the repair of the largest siege gun the Allies possessed, a huge gun which fired a 64lb shot. After continuing with a few snippets of news and further information, he was disturbed from his writing by a large explosion. Returning to his letter later he added some important news:

> Since my writing thus much Manchester played his mine with very good success, made a fair breach, and entered with his men and possessed the manor house [King's Manor], but Leven and Fairfax not being acquainted therewith, that they might have diverted the enemy at other places, the enemy drew all their strength against our men, and beat them off again, but with no great loss, as I hear.

With these few words Sir Henry summed up the events of the day. St Mary's Tower, and the wall adjacent to it, lay in ruins, and the breach had been assaulted, won and then lost again. Why had only one mine been exploded, and how had the assault been stopped?

St Olave's Church, used as an observation post.

The mine under St Mary's Tower seems to have been blown without any warning to the other commanders. Simeon Ashe intimates that Manchester's men had no choice but to blow it when they did:

> Upon the sixteenth day, the Earl of Manchester's men (having by many days labour undermined a tower belonging to the Manor near Bootham Bar) were compelled to spring the mine, for that work could not longer be delayed, in regard of waters which increased upon them, in the chamber of the mine.

This is a perfectly feasible excuse for springing the mine at very short notice. Several contemporary accounts talk of the inclement weather in June 1644, with heavy rains on and off throughout the month. Ashe was a close associate of the Earl of Manchester and would probably have been aware of the reason for exploding the mine. This is also supported by a Royalist source, Sir Henry Slingsby:

> The Scots [Sir James Lumsden's men with Fairfax] were all the while busy about the mine, and we as busy in countermining, but at length both give over being hindered by water.

Although Slingsby is writing about the mine at Walmgate Bar, his comments support Ashe's assertion that the mine was blown early because it was in the process of flooding. On the other hand Sir Thomas Fairfax ascribes the blowing of the mine to much more base reasons:

> Till, in my Lord Manchester's quarters, approaches were made to St Mary's Tower; and soon came to mine it; which Colonel Crawford, a Scotchman, who commanded that quarter, (being ambitious to have the honour, alone, of springing the mine) undertook, without acquainting the other Generals with it, for their advice and concurrence, which proved very prejudicial.

Laurence Crawford was the commander, or Major-General, of the Earl of Manchester's foot, and his men carried out the assault on the King's Manor. Whatever the reason was for exploding the mine, a large breach was created in the wall of the King's Manor, and the attack began.

The King's Manor was a walled area outside the city walls, containing the manor house, the ruins of St Mary's Abbey, destroyed during the Reformation, and St Olave's Church. It is interesting to note that if Crawford's men had successfully taken the manor, they would still have been outside the main city walls.

The Earl of Manchester gives a strength of 600 men to the assault force, and these men used a combination of the breach and ladders against the adjacent walls to cross into the manor. Directly inside the wall was a bowling green, which still exists today, and the Royalist commander in the area, Sir Phillip Byron, was killed as he opened a door to this green. Crawford's men continued their attack, crossing several walls within the manor, and penetrating some way into the defences.

The Royalists seem to have reacted very quickly, and were able to defend the breach in strength. Newcastle personally led a body of 80 men from his own regiment, the Whitecoats. The defenders do not seem to have attempted to drive the enemy back through the breach, but to cut them off from it, stopping the enemy reinforcing their attack and forcing the attackers who had penetrated to surrender.

Bowling Green, looking towards St Mary's Tower. The breach was beyond the tree.

St Mary's Abbey.

The fight was over quickly, and the ground within the manor was littered with Parliamentary dead, 'as might be seen in the bowling green, orchard and garden', as Sir Henry Slingsby put it. Simeon Ashe initially gave their casualties as between 12 and 20 men killed and 200 taken prisoner, but revised this figure in a second letter several days later:

> About 15 of our men were slain within the city, and 20 at the most without the walls; well nigh 40 were wounded without the town, and about 60 (as we hear) within, who together with an hundred more were taken prisoners.

Ashe goes on to say that the enemy's loss was greater than theirs, as they had been informed by people escaping from the town. The Parliamentary losses were confirmed in a letter from the Earl of Manchester to the Committee of Both Kingdoms:

> Yesterday within my quarters I sprang a mine, which did great execution upon the enemy, blowing up a tower which joined to the Manor yard, and this mine taking so great effect my Major-General commanded 600 men to storm the Manor house, who beat the enemy and took 100 prisoners, but, being over confident, 2,000 of the enemy's best men fell upon them and beat them back. I lost near 300 men, but still maintain the breaches and the enemy dare not make any sally out; we are now so near them that we are very ill neighbours one to another.

On 17 June Manchester's men heard the cries of the wounded, both Royalist and Parliamentary, still lying within the ruins of the tower and around the breach. They immediately began to dig and recovered two people alive and one dead before they were stopped by fire from the city, the Royalists still being nervous of another attack. It was not until 19 June that permission was given for the Parliamentary

King's Manor –
side view.

King's Manor –
front view.

army to recover the bodies of their dead comrades for burial.

With the failure of Crawford's attack the siege ground to a halt, with both sides holding their breath in anticipation as Prince Rupert began his approach march. The next event of note was initiated by the defenders, when, in the early hours of 24 June, a large body of musketeers sallied out of Monks Bar to attack Manchester's quarters. They had little success, and were quickly driven back into the city, having lost 20 killed and another 20 as prisoners.

On 30 June firm intelligence reached the Allied commanders that Prince Rupert had reached Knaresborough, a day's march from York. Rather than have Rupert arrive while their army was spread around the city, it was decided that the army would march early on 1 July, gathering at Hessay, to the west of York, which stood on Rupert's direct route from Knaresborough, via Wetherby. There the Allied army formed in line of battle and awaited the Prince's arrival.

On 16 May Prince Rupert began his move north. For several months he had been receiving letters urging him to provide aid to the King's beleaguered northern armies, in Lancashire and Yorkshire. The Earl of Derby wrote to the Prince in

March to ask him for aid in relieving Lathom House, in Lancashire, where his wife was besieged, the local Royalists being unable to provide assistance as they were still trying to recover from their defeat by Sir Thomas Fairfax at Nantwich earlier in the year. Of more relevance to the war in Yorkshire were two letters written by the Marquess of Newcastle towards the end of March. In the first, written on the 25th, the Marquess stated:

> That if your Highness do no please to come hither, and that very soon too, the great game of your uncle's [the King] will be endangered, if not lost; and with your Highness being near, certainly won.

The second letter, written on the 29th, followed in a similar vein:

> Could your Highness march this way it would, I hope, put a final end to our troubles: but I dare not urge this, but leave it to your Highness's great wisdom.

Other letters mention messages being passed by word of mouth, and it would be intriguing to know what these verbal communications were, and to have the Prince's whole correspondence for the period leading up to his march north.

Such a march north also made perfect strategic sense. Early in the war Lancashire had been a fertile recruiting ground for the King's cause, but after the battle of Sabden Brook in May 1643, which gave control of most of the county to Parliament, this source of recruits dried up. An attack into Lancashire would almost certainly relieve Lathom House, the only remaining Royalist outpost, and had a very good chance of relieving York, by drawing part, or all, of the Allied army over the Pennines. As has already been mentioned, Parliament urged the Allied commanders, on several occasions, to follow exactly this course of action,

Bootham Bar from High Petergate. Bootham and St Mary's Tower lie beyond the gate.

but, much to their credit, they refused to be drawn.

By 23 May the Prince, gathering troops to him as he marched, including Sir John Byron's Cheshire forces, had reached Knutsford. He rested his army for a day, having marched for four consecutive days in bad weather. At this point several sources, both Royalist and Parliamentary, give a similar strength for the Prince's army – 2,000 horse and 6,000 foot. Rupert had a major obstacle between his forces and Lancashire, the River Mersey, which could only be crossed in three places between the sea and Manchester: Hale Ford, Warrington and Stockport. On 25 May Rupert's men forced a crossing at the latter, driving the town's locally raised garrison before them. The Parliamentary troops seem to have taken to their heels very quickly, one source even reporting that there were no casualties on either side.

The immediate effect of Rupert's entry into Lancashire was the withdrawal of the forces besieging Lathom House. Colonel Rigby, the Parliamentary commander at Lathom, withdrew his 2,000 men into Bolton, and became an immediate target for the Prince's army. The storming of Bolton is one of the blackest incidents of the whole Civil Wars, if Parliamentary propaganda is to be believed, but there is some reason to doubt the events they report.

Colonel Rigby had his 2,000 men and between 500 and 1,500 clubmen, depending on which source is believed, with which to garrison the town. On 28 May Rupert's army, grown to between 10,000 and 12,000 men by an accession of Lancashire recruits, approached Bolton. Rigby's men awaited them, manning the hedges, buildings and the barricades at the street ends, and Rupert's first attack was repulsed after hard fighting. Now occurred an incident, which caused the Royalist blood to boil, and was a major contributing factor to what happened later. Prince Rupert's diary reports that 'During the time of the attack they took a prisoner (an Irishman) and hung him up as an Irish Papist.'

There is a very good chance that this is true. Part of Sir John Byron's forces had returned from Ireland, and could have recruited native Irishmen while they were there, and one of these regiments had taken part in the first attack. What is more interesting is that the same incident is reported in a Parliamentary source. John Rushworth, who was a secretary in Parliament, states:

> That the Prince sending an Officer to summon the town, they not only refused, but in defiance caused one of the Prince's Captains whom they had taken not long before, to be hanged in his sight.

Bolton's defenders must have been very sure of themselves to carry out such an act in full view of the Royalist army.

His blood up, Rupert ordered a second attack, which succeeded, possibly with the help of a local inhabitant who showed the attackers an unguarded entrance into the town, and the Royalist troops let loose their anger. The town was plundered and its defenders and inhabitants chased through the surrounding countryside, and cut down wherever they were found. A Parliamentary source, Simeon Ashe, reports 1,500 dead being buried in the two days after the assault, but this evidence is not borne out by the Parish Register, which lists only seventy-eight names, including two women. This seems a surprisingly low figure, and casts doubt on the veracity of the Parliamentary accounts.

York Minster – front elevation.

Rupert rested his men on 29 May before moving on to Bury on the 30th, where he received a welcome reinforcement, the Northern Horse. Having marched through the Midlands, and being joined by their old commander, George Goring, recently released from captivity after his capture at Wakefield, they followed the Prince into Lancashire, where their 3,000 troopers were a great boon to him. Sir John Meldrum, who had been despatched with reinforcements to Manchester, gave the strength of the Prince's army on 31 May as 4,000 horse and 7,000 foot, but then mentions the Northern Horse as a separate body, giving the Prince a total of 7,000 horse and 7,000 foot.

Rupert's next objective was Liverpool, which would provide the Royalists with a good port for the arrival of reinforcements from Ireland. On 4 June the Royalists left Bury and, marching via Bolton and Wigan, arrived at Liverpool on the 7th. The garrison of 600 men, including a number of sailors from the ships in the port, was commanded by Colonel Moore, who promptly refused Prince Rupert's summons to surrender the town. Between the 7th and the 9th the Royalists bombarded the town's walls, and by the 10th the defences had been reduced enough for the Royalists to attempt an assault, which was repulsed by Moore's men, after an hour's hard fighting. Moore realised that the town was untenable, and during the night withdrew his men, complete with their arms, ammunition, and artillery, onto the ships anchored in the port. Early on 11 June Colonel Henry Tillier, one of Rupert's regimental commanders, realised what was going on and led his men into the town, where the few remaining defenders, mainly stragglers, were put to the sword.

While Rupert remained at Liverpool, the Committee of Both Kingdoms put plans in place to gather an army in Lancashire to oppose Rupert, and troops from as far afield as Cheshire, Nottinghamshire and Shropshire were ordered to march to Manchester and join with Sir John Meldrum's forces, under the command of the Earl of Denbigh. These troops would take so long to come together that they would have little effect on the campaign.

During Rupert's stay at Liverpool he received a letter from his uncle, the King, which has been a source of heated debate ever since. Rupert interpreted the letter as a direct command to fight the Allied army at York, and stated as much to the Marquess of Newcastle early on the day of the battle of Marston Moor. The letter is open to a number of interpretations, but Rupert genuinely seems to have believed that it was an order to fight, and he carried the letter with him to his dying day.

With a firm decision made to march to the relief of York, and to engage the enemy army thereabouts, Rupert began a rapid march across the Pennines. Rather than cross one of the more southerly passes, Rupert decided to swing north and cross to Skipton, a strong Royalist garrison, which would cover his march. Leaving Liverpool on 20 June, the Royalist army had reached Preston by the 23rd, and Skipton Castle by the 26th, where the whole army gathered, Goring and his men having crossed the Pennines further north. As has already been mentioned, by the 30th Rupert's army had reached Knaresborough. In a rapid flank march Rupert had completely wrong-footed the Allied cavalry guarding the southern Pennine passes, and was within a day's march of York. His obvious route to York was along the south side of the Ouse via Wetherby, and the Allied army had marched from its siege lines to Hessay on 1 July to block the Prince's advance. Yet again the Prince fooled his opponents, by marching via Boroughbridge, along the north side of the Ouse, sending a body of cavalry along the Wetherby road to pin his opponents in place. By the night of 1 July the Prince's army was camped in the Forest of Galtres, to the north-west of York, and had captured a bridge of boats across the Ouse. York had been relieved.

CHAPTER XI

'God made them stubble to our swords'
– the Battle of Marston Moor

In Marston corn fields falls to singing psalms. Sir Henry Slingsby

By nightfall on 1 July, the two armies lay within a few miles of one another, separated by the River Ouse. In the Allied camp a council of war was held during the night to decide what should be done on the morrow, and Thomas Stockdale reported its results in a letter to Parliament:

> Upon this the generals and principal field officers held another consultation upon Monday at night, wherein it was resolved the next morning to rise from thence, and march to Cawood, Tadcaster, and those parts, from whence they could not only safeguard the forces from Cheshire etc, but also prevent the marching of Prince Rupert southwards, and likewise (by the help of a bridge of boats then at Cawood) to stop all provisions going to York either from the West or East Riding, and so in time necessitate his to draw out and fight.

Sir John Meldrum was on the march from Manchester with a sizeable force, at least 4,000 horse and 4,000 foot. By withdrawing to the south the Allied army would cover this force's crossing of the Pennines, and receive a major reinforcement. The Allied commanders were also working under the impression that Prince Rupert's force was at least 25,000 men strong, equalling if not exceeding their own combined forces. In fact Rupert only had about 14,000 men. The Prince's reputation, and the supposed size of his army, which could now be reinforced by Newcastle's men, brought the Allied commanders to a decision to withdraw, although this decision may not have been unanimous, as Sir Thomas Fairfax reports:

> We were divided in our opinions what to do. The English were for fighting them; the Scots, for retreating, to gain (as they alleged) both time and place of advantage.

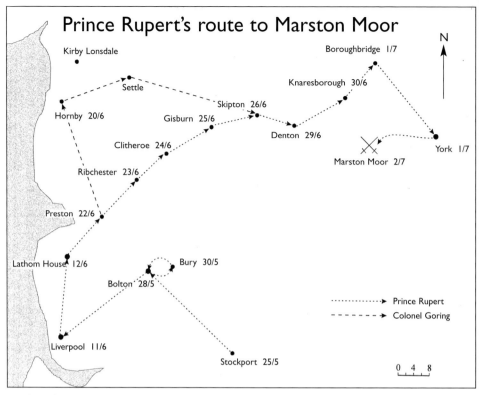

Prince Rupert's route to Marston Moor

N

Kirby Lonsdale

Boroughbridge 1/7

Settle

Knaresborough 30/6

Skipton 26/6

Hornby 20/6

Gisburn 25/6

Denton 29/6

Clitheroe 24/6

York 1/7

Marston Moor 2/7

Ribchester 23/6

Preston 22/6

Lathom House 12/6

Bury 30/5

Bolton 28/5

Prince Rupert
Colonel Goring

Liverpool 11/6

Stockport 25/5

0 4 8

Sir Thomas makes this sound like a minor strategic disagreement, but another source, Thomas Fuller, shows that these disagreements may have gone much deeper:

> Such were the present animosities in the Parliament's Army, and so great their mutual dissatisfactions when they drew off from York, that (as a prime person since freely confessed) if let alone, they would have fallen foul amongst themselves, had not the Prince preparing to fight them, cemented their differences to agree against a general enemy.

If the Allied army had been left alone, according to Fuller, they would have fallen out and separated, but Rupert was not the type of commander to tamely allow an enemy to withdraw, particularly when he had a direct order to fight, all the excuse he needed.

No such prevarications existed among the Royalist command. Rupert had decided to advance across the Ouse, using the bridge of boats his men had captured and a nearby ford. He also sent peremptory orders to York, commanding Newcastle to meet him on Marston Moor at first light, with all his men. This must have rankled, since Newcastle had been an independent commander since the start of the war. In reality, Prince Rupert was senior to Newcastle in the Royalist hierarchy, and was within his rights to give the Marquess orders, but, as a sop to Newcastle's sensibilities, George Goring, who had been the commander of Newcastle's horse until his capture at Wakefield, carried the order.

Early on the morning of 2 July, the Allied army began its march towards Tadcaster, having left a body of 3,000 horse and dragoons, commanded by Oliver

Cromwell, Sir Thomas Fairfax and David Leslie, Leven's Lieutenant-General, to form a rearguard. The Royalists were also on the move early on the 2nd, and the waiting Allied rearguard, posted on the ridge above Long Marston village, soon noticed large bodies of enemy horse deploying onto the open moor below them, which were quickly followed by regiments of foot, and the whole began to form for battle. Thomas Stockdale writes:

> Where about 9 o'clock in the morning they discovered that the enemy had drawn over a great part of their army by a bridge they surprised the night before, and a ford near to it. Whereupon the generals gave present order to call back the foot with the ordnance, ammunition, and carriages.

Unfortunately, by the time the recall order was issued the vanguard of the Scots foot had almost reached Tadcaster, and the army would take some considerable time to return to the field and deploy.

On the moor, Prince Rupert was having similar problems. Newcastle had been ordered to arrive, with all his infantry, by four o'clock, but at nine there was still no sign of him. While Rupert waited he decided to attempt to gain an advantage over his opponents, by capturing the western end of the ridge upon which the Allied rearguard was deployed. Captain William Stewart, a Parliamentary officer, reported the results of this skirmish:

> In the meanwhile, the enemy perceiving that our cavalry had possessed themselves of a corn hill, and having discovered near unto that hill a place of great advantage, where they might have both sun and wind of us, advanced thither with a regiment of Red Coats and a party of horse; but

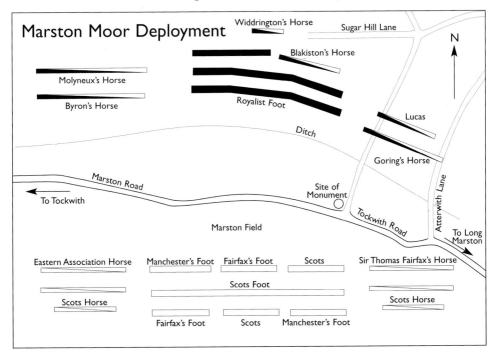

Marston Moor Deployment

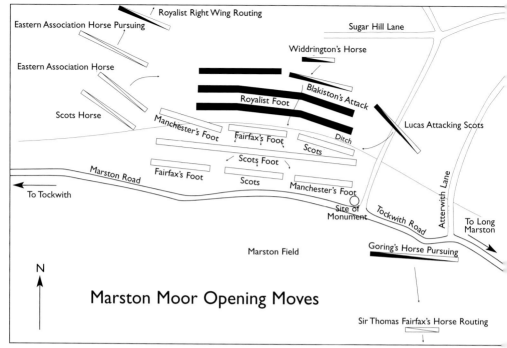

Royalist Right Wing Routing

Eastern Association Horse Pursuing

Sugar Hill Lane

Eastern Association Horse

Widdrington's Horse

Scots Horse

Royalist Foot

Blakiston's Attack

Manchester's Foot

Fairfax's Foot

Ditch

Lucas Attacking Scots

Scots

Scots Foot

Fairfax's Foot

Scots

Marston Road

Manchester's Foot

To Tockwith

Site of Monument

Tockwith Road

Atterwith Lane

To Long Marston

Marston Field

Goring's Horse Pursuing

N

Marston Moor Opening Moves

Sir Thomas Fairfax's Horse Routing

we understanding well their intentions, and how prejudicial it would be unto us if they should keep that ground, we sent out a party which beat them off, and planted our left wing of horse.

The area of the skirmish was almost certainly Bilton Bream, above Tockwith village, as it was in this area that the Allied left wing, commanded by Oliver Cromwell, was deployed later in the day.

At about this time the Earl of Newcastle arrived on the field with his newly raised bodyguard troop, formed of 'gentlemen of quality which were in York', but none of his foot. The Prince expressed his regret that Newcastle's men had not arrived, and Newcastle explained that his men had been busy pillaging the abandoned enemy siege lines, and could not be gathered in time to march. His Lieutenant-General, James King, Lord Eythin, was busy gathering them together, and would arrive in due time. This could have not inspired Rupert with much confidence, as Rupert and King had crossed each other's paths several years earlier, during the Thirty Years War in Germany. At the Battle of Vlotho Rupert had

Marston Moor panorama – looking from Allied lines toward Royalist positions.

ROYALIST ARMY

Horse

led the Protestant horse in an unsuccessful attack, and had been captured and imprisoned. Rupert blamed King for his imprisonment, as King had not supported Rupert's horsemen with his foot soldiers, and King blamed Rupert for his impetuous charge. There was no love lost between the pair.

By two o'clock both armies were deployed ready for battle, although there is some evidence that Newcastle's foot did not arrive from York until nearer four. At two o'clock the first shots of the battle were fired by the Allied artillery.

The battlefield lay between two villages, Long Marston in the east and Tockwith in the west. A road now runs between them, and to its south the ground rises quite steeply to a ridge, 38 metres high at its highest point. Most of the ridge stands at about 30 metres, and it was from this ridge that the Allied rearguard watched Rupert's army deploy onto the moor below, and along it that the Allied army initially formed its battle lines. At the western end of the ridge, close to Tockwith, is Bilton Bream, which included a hedged rabbit warren that provided the people of Tockwith with a supply of meat throughout the year. As the Eastern Association horse deployed into this area, pioneers were tasked with clearing these hedges, which would restrict the horse's ability to deploy, and its movement once battle had been joined.

The ridge between the two villages was covered by a large cornfield, which ran beyond the road to the edge of the moor. Between the cultivated land and the moor lay an obstacle, variously described as a ditch or a hedge, which varied in extent along its length. Towards Tockwith, in front of Cromwell's Eastern Association horse, the obstacle seems to have comprised a small ditch and bank. Next in line were Lawrence Crawford's Eastern Association foot, and the obstacle here was negligible, if it existed at all. A hedge or a ditch, a hedge in front of Lord Fairfax's foot and a ditch in front of the Scots, faced the rest of the Allied infantry front line. In front of Sir Thomas Fairfax's wing the cultivated land ended in a six-foot bank, dropping down onto the moor, which also seems to have been more rugged, with 'whins and ditches' that caused Fairfax's men many problems. As can be seen from the description, the obstacle does not seem to have formed one continuous unbroken line, with different areas being more easy or difficult to cross. There is also evidence that a number of small enclosures existed along the ditch/hedge.

The Royalist army deployed on the uncultivated land to the north of the obstacle. This was ideal terrain to fight a battle, level and gently sloping – the moor drops only eight metres in 1,000 from the bottom of the ridge across the moor. To the rear of the Royalist position was a large wood, which still exists today, Wilstrop Wood. This marked the northern edge of the battlefield.

Tockwith looking towards the Royalist right wing of horse.

Several tracks ran across the field. Moor Lane, which still runs north from the monument, crosses the ditch after about 400 metres and then continues for 600 metres further until it comes to a crossroads. Turning east at this point, the track continued towards Hessay and back towards York, and it is probable that this was the route taken by Newcastle's foot, as they marched to the battlefield from York. It was also the escape route for many of the routing Royalist troops at the end of the day. Local children still dare one another to venture down this lane at night. From the crossroads another track continued north, although this track no longer exists. Sugar Hill Lane runs west from the crossroads for about 600 metres, until it reaches a small field called White Syke Close. For a long time this close has been identified as the location of one of the battle's most poignant events, which will be discussed later, but it did not exist at the time of the battle, and did not come into existence until the moor was enclosed during the late 18th century. Another track, Atterwith Lane, ran north across the moor from the western edge of Long Marston.

Initially, the Allied army formed on the ridge between Long Marston and Tockwith, with two wings of horse and the foot in the centre. Sir Thomas Fairfax commanded the right wing of horse, which comprised 3,000 horse and 500 dragoons from Lord Fairfax's Northern Army, 500 commanded musketeers, and 1,000 Scottish horse, in three regiments. Sir Thomas commanded the first line in person, and this was divided into five bodies of approximately 300 men each, interspersed with small bodies of commanded shot, about 50 musketeers in each. The second line was of a similar size and composition, and was commanded by John Lambert. In reserve were the three regiments of Scottish horse, each approximately 300 men strong, commanded by the Earl of Eglinton, from left to right: Balgonie, Eglinton, and Dalhousie. Balgonie's regiment was unique on the battlefield, as half its men were armed with lances, and the regiment fought as two squadrons, one of lancers, the other of normal troopers.

Massed in the centre of the Allied line were the regiments of foot, 15,000–16,000 strong. The first line was made up of five brigades, each formed of two bodies, or in the case of the Scots, regiments. The right of the line was formed by two brigades of Scots, the first made up of the regiments of Maitland and Crawford-Lindsay, and the second of Rae and Hamilton. Next, forming the centre of the line, was a brigade of Lord Fairfax's Northern Foot. Identification of the regiments that made up the two bodies is problematic to say the least. Many of Fairfax's regiments were well under strength, and the two bodies comprising this brigade could have been formed from several regiments each. The left of the first line was formed by two brigades of the Earl of Manchester's Eastern Association foot, commanded by Lawrence Crawford, each of two bodies. Once again it is difficult to allocate individual regiments.

The Allied second line comprised four brigades, all of them formed from Scots regiments. From right to left these were: Loudon, Buccleuch, Cassillis, Kilhead, Dunfermline, Coupar, Livingstone and Yester. The third line was once again made up of four brigades. As with the front line, it had units from all three armies, with a brigade of Manchester's foot forming the right, a Scots brigade comprising the regiments of Dudhope and Erskine, and two brigades of Lord Fairfax's foot. Finally, two late-arriving Scots regiments formed a short fourth line, although the names of these regiments are not known.

The Allied left wing of horse was commanded by Oliver Cromwell, and comprised 3,000 of the Earl of Manchester's horse, 1,000 Scots horse, 500 commanded musketeers, and at least 500 dragoons. Cromwell commanded the first line, with five bodies of horse, approximately 300 men each, interspersed with bodies of 50 commanded shot. At the western end of this line was Frazer's regiment of Scots dragoons. Colonel Bartholomew Vermuyden commanded the second line, again of five bodies of horse, interspersed with musketeers. The Eastern Association is known to have had a regiment of dragoons, five companies strong, commanded by John Lilburne. This regiment is not mentioned in contemporary accounts of the battle, but probably formed on the left of Vermuyden's second line, and operated in support of Frazer's Scots dragoons. Finally, David Leslie, the Earl of Leven's Lieutenant-General, formed a third line with the regiments of Balcarres, Kirkcudbright, his own.

As can be seen from the above description, the Allied army was formed in the textbook manner, with infantry in the centre and cavalry on the wings. This does not seem to have been the case with the Royalist army.

John Byron commanded the Royalist right wing, which had a strength of 3,000 horse and 500 commanded musketeers. Byron commanded the first line, which was formed from his own regiment, and those of Sir John Urry, Sir William Vaughan and Colonel Marcus Trevor. Lord Molyneux, who commanded his own regiment as well as those of Sir Thomas Tyldesly, Colonel Thomas Levenson, and Prince Rupert, led Byron's second line. Between the two lines of horse was Colonel Samuel Tuke's regiment, whose mission was to protect the open right flank of the Royalist horse. Between

Marston Moor monument.

The ditch looking from Moor Lane towards Tockwith. Close to this spot two Scots foot regiments held their position against several attacks by horse and foot.

Vaughan and Trevor's regiments was a sizeable gap. Filling this gap, but not part of Byron's command, was a brigade of foot, formed by Prince Rupert's blue-coated regiment and Byron's. It is difficult to establish why this brigade was positioned well away from the remainder of the Royalist foot. There are several possible reasons. First, that these regiments had supported the Royalist horse's attempt to take the Bilton Bream during the morning, and had not been pulled back to form up with the rest of the foot. Second, that the brigade had been moved forward to support some Royalist guns, which could have been a contributory factor to the battle starting when it did. Third, the brigade may have been positioned deliberately to protect a gap in the hedge and ditch line, where in due course Crawford led his men through. Whether any one of these reasons, or a combination, is correct, the brigade was out on a limb, with little support once the battle started.

The Royalist centre was formed of a mixture of horse and foot, and Rupert may have been forced to deploy several units of horse to support his thin infantry line

The pond close to the ditch and Moor Lane. One possible site of the Whitecoats' last stand.

while he awaited the arrival of Newcastle's foot from York. The centre comprised approximately 10,000 foot and 1,200 horse. The first line was made up of a number of the regiments with which Rupert had marched from Lancashire, from right to left: Warren, Tyldesly, Broughton, Erneley and Gibson (two weak regiments forming one body) and Tillier, the whole commanded by Colonel Henry Tillier, a veteran of the wars in Ireland. Initially, only the left half of the second line was formed, with space on the right for Newcastle's men to fill once they arrived. Once again, the regiments forming the left half of the second line all belonged to Prince Rupert's army, and were formed of the regiments of Cheater and Chisenhall, with a small body of Derbyshire foot in between. Newcastle's foot filed into position to the right of the line, with three bodies of foot forming part of the second line, and four further bodies forming a short third line. It is very difficult to ascertain which regiments were involved, and Newcastle's 3,500-strong foot was made up of many small, under-strength regiments.

Behind the centre of the Royalist foot was Sir William Blakiston's brigade of horse, about 500 men strong. Further to the rear was another brigade of horse, about 400 men, commanded by Sir Edward Widdrington, and close by was Prince Rupert's Lifeguard and a small body of horse commanded by George Porter. One final body of horse was somewhere in this area, the Marquess of Newcastle's Lifeguard, formed that morning from gentlemen volunteers in York. Although it is not known exactly where this troop was deployed, it certainly fought in this area of the battlefield.

Colonel George Goring, a brilliant if somewhat erratic commander, commanded the Royalist left wing – Marston Moor was to prove one of his better days. It had a similar strength to the Royalist right wing, approximately 3,000 horse and 500 musketeers. Its front line was formed from the regiments of Colonels John Frescheville and Rowland Eyre, and Sir Marmaduke Langdale's brigade, and was commanded by Goring in person. Sir Charles Lucas commanded the second line, which was formed from Sir Richard Dacre's brigade of horse. Finally, Colonel Francis Carnaby's regiment was deployed between the two lines to protect their flanks, much as Tuke's regiment was on the right flank. The Royalists also deployed small bodies of musketeers along the length of the ditch and hedge, to provide warning of an Allied advance and oppose their crossing of the obstacle.

At about two o'clock the first shots of the battle were fired, as Leonard Watson, Manchester's scout master, writes:

> About two of the clock, the great ordnance of both sides began to play, but with small success to either; about five o'clock we had a general silence on both sides, each expecting who should attack first.

Other contemporary writers agree with Watson about the start of the bombardment and its general lack of effect. The slow, steady, bombardment continued until about five o'clock, when silence fell once again over the field. Few casualties are reported, but several individuals are named. For example, Sir Henry Slingsby reports the death of Captain Haughton, son of Sir Gilbert Haughton, and this occurred early enough in the bombardment for Haughton's body to be

Sir Thomas Fairfax's Horse

Panorama – looking through the Royalist lines towards the ridge.

returned to York for burial. Oliver Cromwell also reported the death of his nephew, Captain Valentine Walton, to his father:

> Sir, God hath taken away your eldest son by a cannon-shot. It broke his leg. We were necessitated to have it cut off, whereof he died.

Simeon Ashe also reports an incident, related to him by Lord Grandison, a Royalist officer captured after the battle:

> Before the fight, while the cannon was playing on both sides, a trooper hearing the singing of psalms in our several regiments [Manchester's], came three times to his Lordship with bloody oaths and fearful execrations in his mouth, telling him, that the Roundheads were singing psalms, and therefore they should be routed that day, and that himself should be slain. His Lordship did reprove him, and cane him for swearing and cursing, but he proceeded in his wickedness; and as these words, God damn me, God sink me, were in his mouth, a drake bullet [cannonball] killed him.

The Allied troops singing psalms is also reported by Sir Henry Slingsby, who writes that they 'in Marston fields falls to singing psalms'.

Neither army seemed to be keen on attacking the other, and a long pause ensued. During this pause a discussion took place between the Royalist commanders, James King, Lord Eythin, having arrived from York. As has already been mentioned, there was no love lost between Rupert and King, and Sir Henry Slingsby reports their discussions:

> The Prince demanded of King how he liked the marshalling of the army, who replied he did not approve of it being drawn too near the enemy, and in a place of disadvantage, then said the Prince 'they must be drawn to a further distance.' 'No Sir' said King 'it is too late.' It is so, King dissuaded the Prince from fighting, saying 'Sir your forwardness lost us the day in Germany, where yourself was taken prisoner,' upon the dissuasions of the Marquess and King and that it was near night, the Prince was resolved not to join battle that day, and therefore gave order to have provisions for his army brought from York, and did not imagine the enemy durst make

Panorama – looking through the Royalist lines towards the ridge.

Oliver Cromwell's Horse

Allied Foot

any attempt; so that when the alarm was given, he was set upon the earth at meat a pretty distance from his troops, and many horsemen were dismounted and laid on the ground with their horses in their hands.

The Duchess of Newcastle also reports these discussions, and adds that her husband was in his coach resting when the Allied attack commenced.

At some time between five and seven the Allied army had descended from the ridge to within musket shot, a couple of hundred yards, of the Royalist-manned hedge and ditch. At about seven thirty the whole Allied army began to advance. Why did Leven decide to attack so late in the day, with only two to three hours of light left? Sir Hugh Cholmley gives one possible reason:

> The reason why they fell thus suddenly upon the Prince, as many conjecture, is that a Scottish officer amongst the Prince's horse, whilst the armies faced one another, fled to the Parliament army and gave them intelligence; and it was further observed that Hurry a Scotchman having marshalling of the horse in the Prince's right wing, his own troop were the first that turned their backs; yet I have heard the Prince in his own private opinion did not think Hurry capable of infidelity.

There seems to be little evidence to support this claim, and Prince Rupert did not believe Hurry capable of such base treachery.

A much more convincing reason is that given by Edmund Ludlow, who writes that Cromwell:

> Engaged the right wing of the enemy commanded by Prince Rupert, who had gained an advantageous piece of ground upon Marston Moor, and caused a battery to be erected upon it, from which Captain Walton, Cromwell's sister's son, was wounded by a shot in the knee. Whereupon Colonel Cromwell commanded two field pieces to be brought in order to annoy the enemy, appointing two regiments of foot to guard them; who marching to that purpose, were attacked by the foot of the enemy's right wing, that fired upon them from the ditches. Upon this both parties seconding their foot, were wholly engaged, who before had stood only facing each other.

This is a very plausible reason, and quite a few battles throughout history have been started by an over-active subordinate, against the wishes of their commander.

The Royalists had placed several guns in an advantageous position, and had opened fire on Cromwell's horse. Cavalry is hard pushed to stand under artillery fire, so Cromwell ordered a pair of guns forward to engage the enemy cannons. He supported this with two regiments of foot, which were probably from Lawrence Crawford's command, and with his agreement. These regiments were engaged by enemy foot, possibly Rupert's and Byron's regiments. As more troops began to be drawn into the fighting, Leven decided to order the whole army forward, and at about seven thirty the general advance began. Simeon Ashe describes the Allied advance: 'Our Army in its several parts moving down the hill, was like unto so many thick clouds'. As late in the day as it was, both armies prepared to lay on. Leonard Watson also describes the opening of the action:

> About half an hour after seven o'clock at night, we seeing the enemy would not charge us, we resolved by the help of God, to charge them, and so the sign being given, we marched down to a charge. We came down the hill in the bravest order, and with the greatest resolution that was ever seen.

It must have been an awe-inspiring sight: 24,000 men advancing, with colours flying and drums beating.

Initially, the Battle of Marston Moor split into three separate actions, as did many English Civil War battles, with the horse on each wing engaging each other, and the foot closing in the centre. Only when the cavalry actions on the wings were resolved did the remaining horse intervene in the infantry fight.

On the Allied right Sir Thomas Fairfax, and his troopers, were faced by a formidable obstacle, in the form of a steep bank, almost the height of a man, down which they had to descend onto the moor. They had little scope for manoeuvre as to their right was Long Marston, and to the left was the advancing Allied foot. As well as the bank, the cultivated land was separated from the moor by a ditch and a hedge, either side of Atterwith Lane, and both of these obstacles were lined with George Goring's commanded musketeers. Sir Thomas Fairfax, while recounting the lack of success on his wing, describes the terrain and its effects: 'By reason of the whins and ditches which we were to pass over before we could get to the enemy, which put us into great disorder.'

Both Goring and Fairfax had commanded musketeers in support of their mounted men, but while Goring fully exploited his, Fairfax nullified their support by advancing quickly to the attack, out-pacing the musketeers. On the Allied left flank, Cromwell and David Leslie used their dragoons, along with Frazer's and Lilburn's, to clear the Royalist musketeers from the ditch, which then allowed the horse to advance unimpeded. Sir Thomas Fairfax seems to have made no such effort on his wing.

As Sir Thomas's men advanced they were met by a heavy concentration of musket fire from Goring's musketeers, as is shown by recent artefact finds, and hundreds of musket balls have been recovered from the ground over which Sir Thomas had to attack. The Royalist musketeers were able to fire for a longer period than would have been normal because of the slowing effect of the terrain. Once the Parliamentary horse had crossed the obstacle they halted to reform their ranks, but were caught while doing so by the advance of Goring's first line, and had to fight their opponents while they were still in disorder. Sir Thomas takes up the story:

> Notwithstanding, I drew up a body of 400 horse. But because the intervals of horse in this wing only, was lined with musketeers (which did much hurt with their shot) I was necessitated to charge them. We were a long time engaged one with another till, at last, we routed that part of their wing. We charged and pursued them a good way towards York. Myself, only, returned presently, to get the men I left behind me; but that part of the enemy which stood (perceiving the disorder they were in) had charged them, and routed them before I could get to them; so that the good success, we had at first, was eclipsed much by this bad conclusion.

Sir Thomas is in error when he states that only his wing was faced by commanded musketeers, and was probably using it to excuse his defeat. The success of the body under Sir Thomas's command is also mentioned by Captain Stewart, who writes:

> Sir Thomas Fairfax, Colonel Lambert, and Sir Thomas's brother with five or six troops charged through the enemy and went to the left wing of horse.

It seems likely that Sir Thomas's immediate command, almost certainly on the right of the line, a position of seniority, struck Colonel Francis Carnaby's regiment, which was deployed to protect the Royalist flank. If he had attacked Goring's first line he would have then had to face Sir Charles Lucas and the second line, before his men could pursue the routing Royalist troopers towards York, and striking Carnaby's regiment would also have given him some protection from the Royalist musketeers. There is also evidence that Fairfax's men struck the enemy in a more compact and ordered body than the rest of his front line, and one possible reason for this is that Atterwith Lane gave them access to the moor without crossing the bank and ditch.

Stewart seems to have been in error when he reported Lambert being with Sir Thomas and going to Cromwell's wing of the army. Sir Thomas states that 'Colonel Lambert who should have seconded us, but could not get to us charged in another place', and Sir Thomas is also clear that the men who charged with him continued towards York, while he returned to the battlefield alone. Yet again Sir Thomas found himself cut off from his men and surrounded by the enemy:

> But I must not forget to remember with thankfulness God's goodness to me this day, for having charged through the enemy, and my men going after the pursuit, returning back to go to my other troops, I was gotten in among the enemy, which stood up and down the field in several bodies of horse. So, taking the signal out of my hat, I passed through them for one of their own commanders, and got to my Lord Manchester's horse, in the other wing; only with a cut in my cheek, which was given in the first charge; and a shot which my horse received.

The signal Sir Thomas speaks of was a field sign worn by the Allied army, a piece of white paper or handkerchief in the hat band, to differentiate them from the Royalists, the dress and equipment of both sides being so similar. There is evidence, quoted above, to show that Colonel John Lambert, and some of his men, reached Cromwell's flank, but separately to Sir Thomas.

Fairfax had led his men forward and, after a sharp fight, had broken Carnaby's men, pursuing them towards York. Before Sir Thomas could return to the field the remainder of his first line, and the bulk of Lambert's second line, had been driven from the field by George Goring's men. Lambert had managed to avoid the general rout, possibly by following Fairfax through the gap he had created. Sir Thomas, returning to the field, found the rest of his wing in shambles, and at this point he decided to make for the left flank, arriving safely, although he may have left the field shortly after. Simeon Ashe, writing of Sir Thomas's courage, mentions his withdrawal from the field:

> For he stayed in the field until being dismounted and wounded, he was brought off by a soldier. The hurt which Sir Thomas Fairfax received is in his face, but (God be thanked) we fear no danger.

While Fairfax and Lambert had been fighting their way through the Royalist lines, what had been happening to the rest of their men? George Goring had bided his time well, waiting until his musketeers, and the terrain, had disordered the Parliamentary horse, before he launched a shattering counter-charge. Sir Philip Monkton, one of Goring's regimental commanders, describes his experiences during this attack:

> At the battle of Hessay Moor [another name for the battle] I had my horse shot under me as I caracoled at the head of the body I commanded, and so near the enemy that I could not be mounted again, but charged on foot, and beat Sir Hugh Bethell's regiment of horse, who was wounded and dismounted, and my servant brought me his horse. When I was mounted upon him the wind driving the smoke so as I could not see what was become of the body I commanded, which went in pursuit of the enemy.

It is of interest that Sir Philip speaks of charging the enemy on foot, as his horse had been shot, a very brave or foolhardy action. In the time it took him to get remounted his men had disappeared into the distance in pursuit of the broken enemy, which suggests that the fighting was of very short duration. Robert Douglas, the Earl of Leven's chaplain, also reports the brevity of the cavalry action on the Allied right flank, writing 'in the same instant, all Fairfax 3,000 horse fled at once, our horsemen upon that hand stood till they were disordered'. Here Douglas gives another possible reason for Sir Thomas's success, and the failure of the remainder of his wing. While Sir Thomas led the 400 men with him into a charge without waiting to reform, the remainder of the first line did halt to regain their order, and were struck by Goring's men while they were still stationary, a recipe for defeat.

As the two lines of Parliamentary horse were routed, the three regiments of Scottish horse to their rear also had a hard fight of it, as Captain Stewart reports:

> The two squadrons of Balgonie's regiment being divided by the enemy each from the other, one of them being lancers charged a regiment of the enemies foot, and put them wholly to rout, and after joined with the left wing of horse, the other by another way went also to the left wing. The Earl of Eglington's regiment maintained their ground (most of the enemies going in pursuit of the horse and foot that fled) but with the loss of four lieutenants, the lieutenant-colonel, the major, and Eglington's son being deadly wounded.

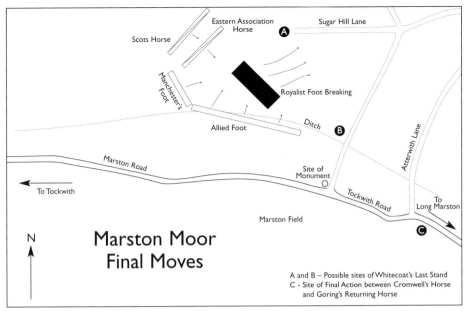

Marston Moor
Final Moves

A and B – Possible sites of Whitecoat's Last Stand
C - Site of Final Action between Cromwell's Horse
and Goring's Returning Horse

Dalhousie's regiment was caught up in the general rout, while Eglington's stood its ground, suffering heavy losses, particularly in officers. The two squadrons of Balgonie's both, separately, made it to the left wing horse, the lancer squadron having broken a regiment of enemy foot on its way. It is likely that this enemy foot was in fact a body of Goring's commanded musketeers, not one of the foot regiments from the centre, as they were covered by the charges of Sir Charles Lucas's men, which will be discussed in due course.

Goring had completely shattered the enemy's right wing, which would play no further part in the battle. While Goring, and his first line, pursued the enemy from the field, Sir Charles Lucas prepared to lead his men into the exposed flank of the Allied centre. Casualties among Fairfax's men were high, and Sir Thomas gives details of the casualties among his officers:

> In which charge also many of my officers were slain, and hurt. The Captain of my own troop was shot in the arm. My Cornet had both his hands cut, which rendered him ever after unserviceable. Captain Micklethwaite, an honest stout man, was slain; and scarce any officer, which was in this charge, which did not receive hurt. But Colonel Lambert who should have seconded us, but could not get to us charged in another place. Major Fairfax who was major to his regiment had at least 30 wounds, whereof he died, after he was abroad, again, and good hopes of his recovery. But that which nearest of all concerned me, was the loss of my brother, who being deserted of his men, was sore wounded, of which, in 3 or 4 days he died. So as, in this charge, as many were hurt, and killed, as in the whole army besides.

Sir Thomas's statement that as many of his men were lost in this one charge, as were killed in the rest of the army during the whole battle, brings home the horror of the action. With the defeat of the Allied right, it is now time to turn to the infantry fight in the centre.

As the Allied foot advanced towards the ditch the Earl of Manchester's regiments, led on by Lawrence Crawford, were the first to make contact. To their front, covering a gap in the ditch, were Prince Rupert and Byron's regiments of foot. Leonard Watson states that Manchester's foot came on at a 'running march', and that 'in a moment we were past the ditch', which supports Stewart's description of the terrain that 'between the Earl of Manchester's foot and the enemy there was a plain', indicating that the obstacle at this point of the line was negligible. Simeon Ashe describes the clash between the two forces:

> Upon the advancing of the Earl of Manchester's foot, after short firings on both sides, we caused the enemy to quit the hedge in a disorderly manner, where they left behind them four drakes.

The Royalist foot was out on a limb, some distance from its nearest supports, and outnumbered, as is described by Thomas Fuller, who writes 'impressed with unequal numbers, and distanced from reasonable succour, became prey to their enemy'. Their only close support was Colonel Marcus Trevor's regiment of horse, which by this time had become involved in the general cavalry mêlée against Cromwell's men. The Royalist foot were soon driven from the meagre shelter of the hedge in some disorder, leaving four guns behind. This then allowed Crawford to exert pressure on the flank of the Royalist foot to his right, which in turn allowed Lord Fairfax's foot to cross the obstacle to their front.

To the right of Crawford's men was a brigade of Lord Fairfax's Northern Foot, and Simeon Ashe writes of their initial success:

> The Lord Fairfax his brigade on our right hand did also beat off the enemy from the hedges before them, driving them from their cannon, being two drakes and one demi-culverin.

As Fairfax's men threw back the enemy infantry, they were counterattacked by a unit of Newcastle's foot, as Simeon Ashe goes on to describe:

> [They were] received by the Marquess of Newcastle's regiment of foot, and by them furiously assaulted, did make a retreat in some disorder.

Newcastle's men, possibly his own regiment, drove Fairfax's brigade back beyond the hedge, in some disorder. To the right of Fairfax's brigade were two brigades of Scots, which formed the right of the Allied foot's first line. They too had managed to cross the obstacle against tough opposition, as William Stewart writes:

> In this ditch the enemy had placed four brigades of their best foot, which upon the advance of our battle [centre] were forced to give ground, being gallantly assaulted by the Earl of Lindsay's regiment, the Lord Maitland's, Cassillis, and Kilhead's. General Major Crawford having overwinged the enemy set upon their flank, and did good execution upon the enemy, which gave occasion to the Scottish foot to advance and pass the ditch.

By this stage the whole of the Allied first line had crossed the obstacle, and were fighting on equal terms on the moor beyond. The only setback had been the repulse of Fairfax's men by Newcastle's, and it was at this moment that disaster struck.

As Lord Fairfax's foot attempted to reform after their repulse they were struck by a body of Royalist horse, in all probability part of Sir William Blakiston's brigade, and Thomas Stockdale describes the effect of this attack on Fairfax's men, and on some of the Scots:

> The Lord Fairfax's foot and Scots that were joined with them pursuing their advantage were charged by the enemy's horse and so disordered that they were forced to fly back and leave our ordinance behind them.

Simeon Ashe supports this statement, as he writes about the repulse of Fairfax's foot, where he adds, 'This advantage espied by a body of the enemy's horse, they charged through them to the top of the hill'. Robert Douglas reports several Scottish regiments from the second line joining in what threatened to become a general rout:

> In this meantime, some of the enemies horse charged the battle, Fairfax brigade of foot fled, the Edinburgh and Artillery regiment followed, first the Chancellor and Maclaines fled, some levy of all the horsemen of the enemy charged up where they were fleeing.

It is sometimes difficult to build a sequence of events for a large battle, as with the relationship between the collapse of the Allied centre and the rout of Sir Thomas Fairfax's horse of the Allied right wing. In this instance it is possible to follow a sequence, as Robert Douglas gives a clue after writing of the collapse of the Allied foot:

> General Leslie [Earl of Leven] came up for horse to beat them in, and went towards the rescue of horse; in that same instant, all Fairfax's 3,000 horse fled at once, our horsemen upon that hand stood till they were disordered.

So, if Douglas's sequence of events is to be believed, and there is no reason for it not to be, Blakiston's counter-attack had broken through Lord Fairfax's foot, with several Scottish regiments getting caught up in the rout. Leven, having seen this, rode towards the right flank to bring up some horse to counter Blakiston's attack, and as he was doing so the Allied right wing horse broke.

There is also some evidence to suggest that the Marquess of Newcastle abandoned his post as an army commander, and led his bodyguard troop forward with Blakiston's men, as his wife reports:

> In this confusion my Lord (accompanied only with his brother Sir Charles Cavendish, Major Scott, Captain Mazine, and his page), hastening to see in what posture his own regiment was, met with a troop of gentlemen volunteers, who formerly had chosen him their captain, notwithstanding he was general of an army; to whom my Lord spoke after this manner 'Gentlemen,' said he, 'you have done me the honour to choose me your captain, and now is the fittest time I may do you service; wherefore if you will follow me, I shall lead you on the best I can, and show you the way to your own honour.' They being as glad of my Lord's proffer as my Lord was of their readiness, went on with the greatest courage; and passing through two bodies of foot, engaged one with each other not at forty yards distance, received not the least hurt, although they fired quick upon

each other; but marched towards a Scots regiment of foot, which they charged and routed; in which encounter my Lord himself killed three with his page's half-leaden sword, for he had no other left him; and though all the gentlemen in particular offered him their swords, yet my Lord refused to take a sword of any of them. At last, after they had passed through this regiment of foot, a pikeman made a stand to the whole troop; and though my Lord charged him twice or thrice, yet he could not enter him, but the troop despatched him soon.

As the broken Allied foot continued to rout towards their baggage train, Blakiston was supported by other bodies of horse and foot, and there was a danger of the Allied army being split in two. However, help was at hand, and Simeon Ashe reports that a body of the Earl of Manchester's foot 'did wheel on their right hand, upon their flank, and gave them so hot a charge, that they were forced to fly back disbanded into the moor'.

The action of Manchester's foot quite probably staved off immediate defeat, but the Allied army was still in grave danger. The survivors of Thomas Fairfax's wing were either pursuing the enemy towards York, or trying to cut their way through to the left wing of the army, while much of the Allied centre's first line, and part of the second, were fleeing southwards. Crawford's men were still making progress against the Royalist foot, but there was then a large gap to the two remaining Scottish regiments in the first line, Maitland and Crawford-Lindsay's. These two regiments were in an unenviable position, with enemy foot to their front, and their right flank exposed by the rout of Sir Thomas Fairfax's men to the remaining Royalist horse, commanded by Sir Charles Lucas, and the Royalists, both horse and foot, began a protracted assault on the two regiments. Sir James Lumsden, who commanded the Scottish foot in the second line, wrote of their extraordinary stand:

> They that fought stood extraordinary well to it, whereof my Lord Lyndsay, his brigade commanded by himself was one.

Captain William Stewart gives more details:

> Sir Charles Lucas and General Major Porter having thus divided all our horse on that wing assaulted the Scottish foot upon their flanks, so that they had foot upon their front, and the whole cavalry of the enemy's left wing to fight with, whom they encountered with so much courage and resolution, that having interlined their musketeers with pikemen they made the enemy's horse, notwithstanding for all the assistance they had of their foot, at two several assaults to give ground; and in this hot dispute with both they continued almost an hour, still maintaining their ground; Lieutenant-General Baillie, and Major-General Lumsden (who both gave good evidence of their courage and skill) perceiving the greatest weight of the battle to lie sore upon the Earl of Lindsay's and Lord Maitland's regiment, sent up a reserve for their assistance, after which the enemy's horse having made a third assault upon them, had almost put them in some disorder; but the Earl of Lindsay, and Lieutenant Colonel Pitscottie, Lieutenant Colonel to the Lord Maitland's regiment, behaved themselves so gallantly, that they

quickly made the enemy's horse to retreat, killed Sir Charles Lucas his horse, took him prisoner and gained ground upon the foot.

The stand of Lindsay's brigade is one of the pivotal moments of the battle, if not the whole 1st Civil War. If these 1,000 Scots had not held their position Lucas's horsemen could have crashed into the flank of the already shaken Allied centre. Baillie and Lumsden eventually led four regiments forward to support Lindsay, and as these regiments advanced Lucas led his troopers forward for the third and final time, during which he was unhorsed and captured.

At this stage of the battle the Royalists had definitely had the better of the fighting, which is reflected in the fact that all three of the Allied commanders, Leven, Fairfax and Manchester, had left, or were in the process of leaving, the field. Leven had withdrawn to either Leeds or Bradford, witnesses state both, and Fairfax had gone to Cawood Castle, near Selby. Manchester was leaving the field when he was confronted by Robert Douglas:

> My Lord Manchester was fleeing with a number of Scots officers. God used me as an instrument to move him to come back again; for I was gathering men a mile from the place, and having some there he drew that way, and having purpose to go away, and some of our officers, as Colonel Lyell, was persuading him to go away, but I exhorted him before many witnesses to go back to the field, and he was induced; we came back about 5 or 600 horse; he only of all the generals was on the field.

All three of the Allied commanders had left the field, although Manchester did return, and would be the only one of the five commanders, on either side, to be on the field at the close of the day. The final phase of the battle would be commanded by the lieutenant-generals, and, fortunately for the Allies, the lieutenant-generals commanding their left wing, Oliver Cromwell and David Leslie, were up to the task, and it was left to this pair to pull victory from the closing jaws of defeat.

As Cromwell and Leslie descended from the Bilton Bream, they faced a similar problem to that faced by Sir Thomas Fairfax, over a mile to their east, although the ditch to their front was not as great an obstacle as that faced by Sir Thomas. They would still have to cross the ditch in the face of John Byron's commanded musketeers, and face Byron's counter charge while still disordered. To counter this, Colonel Fraser's dragoons, possibly supported by Lilburn's, were sent forward to clear the enemy musketeers from the area of the ditch, a task they carried out with few problems, as Captain Stewart reports:

> The Scottish dragoons that were placed upon the left wing, by the good managing of Colonel Frizell [Fraser] acted their part so well, that at the first assault they beat the enemy from the ditch, and shortly after killed a great many, and put the rest to rout.

Fraser's action cleared the way for the Allied horse to cross the ditch unopposed, but before they had the opportunity, fate, and John Byron, took a hand. Rather than waiting for the enemy to cross the ditch, Byron led his first line forward, crossing the ditch himself, as Thomas Fuller reports:

Besides a right valiant Lord, severed (and in some sort secured) with a ditch from the enemy, did not attend till the foe forced their way unto him, but gave his men the trouble to pass over that ditch: the occasion of much disorder.

Although Fuller was not an eyewitness, and wrote his account some time after the event, he asserts that he got his information from 'a prime person' who 'since freely confessed'. Although no other source mentions the crossing of the ditch by the Royalist horse, it could easily account for their rapid defeat. Why did Byron commit himself so quickly? One possible explanation is the effect of the Allied artillery fire on his men, which has already been mentioned. With the start of the action the artillery fire would have intensified, and horse found it very difficult to stand under such fire. The advance of Cromwell's horse gave Byron's troopers an excuse to advance and get clear of the artillery fire.

The clash between the two front lines seems to have been over very quickly, although the evidence is a little contradictory. Sir Henry Slingsby reports:

Cromwell having the left wing drawn into 5 bodies of horse, came off the Coney [rabbit] warren, by Bilton Bream, to charge our horse, and upon their first charge routed them; they fly along by Wilstrop woodside, as fast and as thick as could be.

Oliver Cromwell himself commented that 'we never charged but we routed the enemy', once again pointing to a fairly limited duration to the fighting on his wing. Leonard Watson, on the other hand, reports Cromwell's own unit as having had 'a hard pull of it', being charged in the front and flank by some of Prince Rupert's best troopers, although 'at last (it so pleased God) he brake through them, scattering them before him like a little dust'. Cromwell was slightly wounded during this 'hard pull' and may have left the field for a short time to have his wound dressed, or so Robert Douglas, and local tradition, report.

Several other pieces of evidence point to the whole fight on the Allied left being of short duration. The Duchess of Newcastle writes:

Where upon he [Newcastle] immediately put on his arms, and was no sooner got on horseback, but he beheld a dismal sight of His Majesty's right wing, which out of a panic fear had left the field, and run away with all the speed they could; and though my Lord made them stand once, yet they immediately betook themselves to their heels again, and killed even those of their own party that endeavoured to stop them.

When Newcastle heard the start of the Allied advance he immediately armed himself, and in the time it took him to do this and mount his horse, a matter of minutes, part of the Royalist right wing was routing past him, not to be rallied.

Byron's second line, commanded by Lord Molyneux, may have put up a better performance, and there is evidence that David Leslie's Scots horse had a part in their defeat, as Captain Stewart reports:

He [Leslie] charged the enemy's horse (with whom Lieutenant-General Cromwell was engaged) upon the flank, and in a very short space the enemy's whole cavalry was routed, on whom our fore-troops did execution to the very walls of York; but our body of horse kept their ground.

Cromwell and Leslie kept a major portion of their troops in hand, to fall upon the flanks of the enemy's foot, much as Sir Charles Lucas had done on the other side of the battlefield, where he had been fought to a standstill by Lindsay's brigade of Scots foot. Unfortunately for the Royalists, no such stand would occur until late in the day, when it was too late.

While the fight on the Royalist right was going on, Prince Rupert armed himself and returned to the field, and Sir Hugh Cholmley describes the sight that greeted him:

> Upon the alarm the Prince mounted to horse and galloping up to the right wing, met his own regiment turning their backs to the enemy which was a thing so strange and unusual he said 'swounds, do you run, follow me,' so they facing about, he led them to a charge, but fruitlessly, the enemy having broken the force of that wing, and without any great difficulty, for these troops which formerly had been thought unconquerable, now upon a panic fear, or I know not by what fate, took scare and fled, most of them without striking a stroke, or having the enemy come near them, made as fast as they could to York.

Swounds indeed! Sir Hugh was not an eyewitness, but spoke to senior survivors of the battle the day after when they arrived at Scarborough, and he makes a very interesting point when he states that many of the Royalist horse fled without striking a stroke or being approached by enemy. The defeat of Byron's first line may have swept much of his second line away with it. The attempt to rally his own regiment, which was part of Byron's second line, seems to have been Prince Rupert's only contribution to the battle, other than hiding in a bean field, if Parliamentary propaganda sheets are to be believed, which also take great pleasure in reporting the death of Rupert's favourite dog during the battle. Whatever Rupert's movements were during the remainder of the battle, he had returned to York by eleven o'clock that night.

With the demise of the Royalist right wing, the climax of the battle had been reached, and while Sir Charles Lucas was held at bay by Lindsay's men, Cromwell, Crawford, and David Leslie prepared to fall on the exposed flank of the Royalist centre. There seems to be some debate about exactly what happened next. Many modern authors believe that Cromwell led his men right around the Royalist army to confront George Goring's returning troopers, before falling on the flank of the Royalist infantry. This seems very unlikely, and several contemporary accounts are clear on the course of events. James Somerville writes:

> These two commanders of the horse upon that wing, Leslie and Cromwell wisely restrained the great bodies of their horse from pursuing these broken troops, but wheeling to the left [right] hand, falls in upon the naked flanks of the Prince's main battalion of foot, carrying them down with great violence.

Sir Hugh Cholmley is in agreement:

Those that gave this defeat were most of them Cromwell's horse to whom before the battle were joined David Leslie, and half the Scottish horse; and who kept close together in firm bodies, still falling upon that quarter of the Prince's forces which seemed to make most resistance, which were the foot who fought gallantly and maintained the field three hours after the horse had left them.

Oliver Cromwell himself gives the final piece of evidence:

The left wing, which I commanded, being our own horse, saving a few Scots in our rear, beat all the Prince's horse. God made them stubble to our swords. We charged their regiments of foot with our horse, and routed all we charged.

The attack into the Royalist right flank by Cromwell, Crawford, and Leslie's men seems to have carried all before them, and Leonard Watson describes them 'dispersing the enemy's foot almost as fast as they charged them'. This dispersal of the Royalist foot had one famous exception – the Whitecoats. Newcastle's men brought the Allied advance to a temporary halt, as is described by James Somerville:

Neither met they with any great resistance, until they came to the Marquis of Newcastle his battalion of white coats, who first peppering them soundly with their shot when they came to the charge stoutly bore them up with their pikes, that they could not enter to break them. Here the Parliament horse of that wing received their greatest loss, and a stop for some time to their hoped-for-victory, and that only by the stout resistance of this gallant battalion, which consisted of near four thousand foot, until at length a Scots regiment of dragoons, commanded by Colonel Frizeall [Fraser], with other two, was brought to open them upon some hand, which at length they did; when all their ammunition was spent, having refused quarter, every man fell in the same order and rank wherein he had fought.

The Duchess of Newcastle agrees with Somerville, stating that the Whitecoats 'showed such an extraordinary valour and courage in that action, that they were killed in rank and file'. Sir Henry Slingsby also writes of the Whitecoats' last stand, although his account has a much more personal feel, since he lost two relatives in the action: Colonel John Fenwick, a nephew; and Sir Charles Slingsby, described as a kinsman. Although Fenwick's body could not be identified, Sir Charles's remains were interred in York Minster.

Having been brought to a halt by the Whitecoats, who almost certainly numbered much less than the 4,000 reported, the Allied horse awaited the arrival of Fraser's dragoons, supported by two other units according to Somerville, one of which was probably Lilburne's, although the second remains unidentified. The Royalists had run out of ammunition and were defenceless as Fraser's men pumped musket balls into their packed ranks. Once gaps had appeared, the Allied horse closed for the kill, and an account of these final moments was written by William Lilly, who although not an eyewitness, heard the story from one Captain Camby, who had been one of Cromwell's troopers, and had taken part in the final attack:

Looking from White Syke Close towards Wilstrop Wood. Royalist horse routed from left to right across the southern edge of Wilstrop Wood.

A most memorable action happened on that day. There was one entire regiment of foot belonging to Newcastle, called the Lambs, because they were all clothed in white woollen cloth, two or three days before the fight. This sole regiment, after the day was lost, having got into a small parcel of ground ditched in, and not of easy access of horse, would take no quarter, and by mere valour, for one whole hour, kept the troops of horse from entering amongst them at near push of pike; when the horse did enter, they would have no quarter, but fought it out till there was not thirty of them living; those whose hap it was to be beaten down upon the ground as the troopers came near them, though they could not rise for their wounds, yet were so desperate as to get either a pike or sword, or piece of them, and gore the troopers' horses as they came over them, or passed them by. Captain Camby, then a trooper under Cromwell, and an actor, who was the third or fourth man that entered amongst them, protested, he never in all the fights he was in, met with such resolute brave fellows, or whom he pitied so much, and said, 'he saved two or three against their will'.

Although most accounts, modern and contemporary, are in agreement about the details of the stand, its location is another matter. Three possible sites have been put forward. The traditional one is White Syke Close, although artefact evidence seems to have discredited this. The second, the enclosures on Atterwith Lane, also has little evidence to support it. Finally, the junction of the ditch and Moor Lane, which has recently been put forward as a possible location, and has a large amount of artefact evidence to support it, is a strong contender for the site of the Whitecoats' gallant stand. Until the grave pits where the Whitecoats were buried are discovered, however, it is unlikely that a site for the stand will be proved beyond doubt.

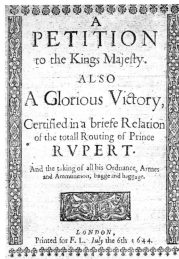

A contemporary tract celebrating the Allied victory at Marston Moor.

With the fall of the Whitecoats the Royalist army disintegrated. Most of the Royalist foot either surrendered or fled back along the lanes towards York, and all that remained for the Allied army to do was pursue the enemy, or so they thought. Several large bodies of Royalist horse, Goring's returning troopers, were forming on the ground upon which Sir Thomas Fairfax had originally deployed. Turning from the destruction of the Royalist foot, Cromwell led his men against the Royalist horse, and in a short, sharp fight saw them off. Simeon Ashe writes about this closing action:

> Yet their horse there still in full bodies; our left wing was neither wearied by their former hot service, nor discouraged by the sight of that strength which yet the enemy had unshaken and entire, but continuing and renewing their valour, they charged every party remaining in the field, till all were fully routed and put to flight: our men pursued the enemy's about three miles, till they came near unto York.

The victorious Allied army had cleared the field. Leonard Watson states that this was achieved by nine o'clock in the evening, which, with the battle starting at around seven or seven thirty, seems a little early, but the pursuit certainly started in daylight, as Captain W.H. reports nightfall bringing an end to it. Some small bodies of Royalist horse remained on the fringes of the battlefield and straggled back to York during the night. The weary Allied soldiers lay down to sleep on the ground on which they had fought and won, but how great a victory had they achieved? Only the morning would tell.

With the exception of the Earl of Manchester, the Allied commanders were unaware of the victory their lieutenants had won. Fairfax received news of the victory while he was at Cawood Castle, and immediately wrote a letter to the mayor of Hull:

> After a dark cloud, it hath pleased God to show the sunshine of his glory, in victory over his enemies, who are driven into the walls of York; many of their chief officers slain, and all their ordnance and ammunition taken, with small loss (I praise God) on our side. This is all I can now write.

This must have come as a great relief to the mayor, as other fugitives from Fairfax's forces had got as far as Hull, and reported an Allied defeat. This news reached London by ship before the true state of affairs, and at least one Parliamentary news tract reported Marston Moor as a defeat.

Royalist losses were severe. Out of an army of 17,000 men, 4,000 had been slain – local inhabitants who buried the bodies reported 4,150 – 2,000 taken prisoner, including Sir Charles Lucas and Major-General Porter, and 5,000 wounded, as individuals escaping from the city reported. Twenty-five cannon, the whole of the Royalist artillery train, had been captured, along with a mass of arms and ammunition.

Allied losses were very light in comparison: not many more than 300 were killed. The Earl of Manchester's foot lost only one officer and six men killed, and a further twenty wounded. Most of the Allied casualties were among the troops who had routed, or were the 'carriage-keepers' on duty when Goring's men pillaged the carriages.

The Allied victory had been greater than they could have ever believed as night fell on 2 July. The Royalists had suffered over 50 per cent losses in dead, wounded and prisoners. Much of the Royalist horse had escaped from the field, but the foot had suffered horrendous losses, with Newcastle's Northern Foot almost ceasing to exist. With the return of Fairfax and Leven to the army, the Allies prepared to return to their siege of York, and put an end to the business.

CHAPTER XII

The fall of York and the end of the campaign in Yorkshire

So that the whole street was thronged up to the bar with
wounded and lame people, which made a pitiful cry among them. Sir Henry Slingsby

A defeated army is never a pretty sight, and the roads between Marston Moor and York were thronged with the detritus of Prince Rupert and Newcastle's army. Bodies of Allied horse pursued the defeated mass almost to the walls of the city, and Sir Thomas Glemham, York's governor, closed the gate to prevent them entering the city along with the fleeing Royalist troops, a wise precaution. Sir Henry Slingsby was caught up in the rout and reported what he found as he approached York:

> At the bar [gate] none was suffered to come in but such as were of the town, so that the whole street was thronged up to the bar with wounded and lame people, which made a pitiful cry among them.

The Marquess of Newcastle arrived at York, accompanied only by his brother and two servants, and there he was met by Prince Rupert and Lord Eythin. The three commanders had much to discuss. Other than a few thousand horsemen their soldiers were either dead, prisoners, or scattered, and the discussion about what to do next went on into the early hours. Rupert seems to have been keen to gather troops and make another attempt to defeat the Allied army, suggesting that he go to North Yorkshire to recruit, while Newcastle would go into County Durham. As well as recruiting troops from these areas, they would be able to receive reinforcements from Lancashire, Westmorland and Cumberland, and act as a rallying point for their defeated troops. Sir Robert Clavering was operating in the north east with a force of several thousand men, and had already started to move south towards York. If Sir Thomas Glemham could hold York for a few weeks, then the Prince was convinced that they could return in strength and defeat the Allies,

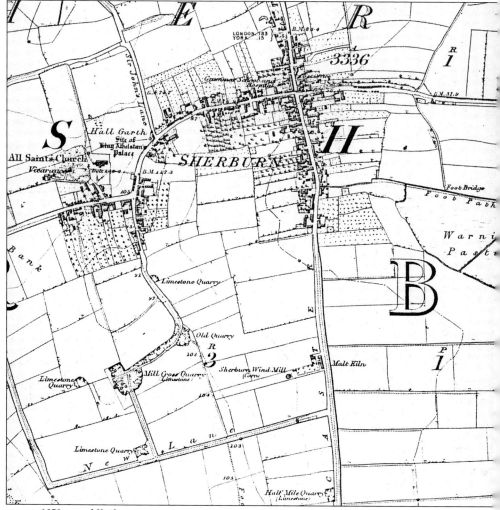

1850 map of Sherburn area.

turning the whole situation in the north on its head.

At first Newcastle seems to have agreed with Prince Rupert's plan, but he changed his mind during the night after further discussions with Lord Eythin, as Sir Hugh Cholmley reports:

> But as is said General King considering the King's affairs absolutely destroyed by the loss of this battle persuaded the Marquess (against all the power of his other friends) to quit the kingdom.

The Duchess of Newcastle also reports Newcastle's decision to leave the country:

> That night my Lord remained in York; and having nothing left in his power to do his Majesty any further service in that kind; for he had neither ammunition, nor money to raise more forces, to keep wither York, or any

other towns that were yet in his Majesty's devotion, well knowing that those which were left could not hold out for long, and being also loath to have aspersions cast upon him, that he did sell them to the enemy, in case he could not keep them, he took a resolution and that justly and honourably, to forsake the kingdom; and to that end, went the next morning to the Prince, and acquainted him with his design, desiring his Highness would be pleased to give this true and just report of him to his Majesty, that he behaved himself like an honest man, a gentleman, and a loyal subject. Which request the Prince having granted, my Lord took his leave.

With this decision made, Rupert and Newcastle parted company and went their separate ways on Wednesday, 3 July.

Newcastle and his entourage left York for Scarborough, escorted by a troop of horse and a company of dragoons provided by Prince Rupert. Two days after his arrival at Scarborough, either the 5 or 6 July, Newcastle boarded ship and sailed to Hamburg, with his two sons and close companions. Eythin may not have been among this number, and there is evidence of a disagreement between him and Newcastle before they set sail on separate ships. Pausing in his pursuit of the Earl of Essex into the West Country, King Charles wrote a touching letter to Newcastle:

My nephew Rupert sends me word of that which troubles me, that you and General King are going or gone beyond the sea. It is a resolution that looks like discontent, which you cannot have occasion for without blemish to that sense which I ought to have of your eminent services, and particularly in your late gallant defence of York; which I would not have you believe that any subsequent ill fortune can lessen, but that I shall ever retain such a memory of that and your other actions of great merit as

Map of Scarborough, from Thomas Jeffreys's The County of York Survey'd, *1775*

ought to be expected from a good master to so deserving a servant. If you persist in that resolution which I cannot but be sorry for, I shall commit the charge of those countries under your command to George Goring and Sir Thomas Glemham, in your absence, who I make no doubt will be the acceptablest persons to you, and who will be likely to give you the best account of their trust at your return, when you shall be sure to be received and ever entertained with that favour and estimation which you may expect. Your most assured constant friend, Charles R.

Newcastle would not return to England until after the Restoration in 1660, and was elevated to a dukedom on his eventual homecoming.

Prince Rupert also left York on 3 July, with a force reported as between 1,500 and 4,000 horse, although the higher figure is more probable, and less than 1,000 foot. By the evening of the 3rd the Prince had reached Thirsk, where he was met by Sir Robert Clavering and his small force, again variously reported as between 1,300 and 2,000 men. From there the combined force marched on to Richmond, where they remained until the 7th, when they departed for Bolton Castle, and it was from there that Rupert wrote a letter to Sir Philip Musgrave, the King's commander in Westmorland and Cumberland, requesting any forces Sir Philip could spare. By 10 July the Prince and his force had crossed the Pennines to Hornby, and would not return to Yorkshire again.

Between 10 and 18 July Rupert marched to and fro in northern Lancashire trying to gain recruits to build his forces for a return to Yorkshire. By the 18th he had reached Kirby Lonsdale, and here news reached him of York's surrender on the 16th, which prompted the Prince to move his forces to the south. By 25 July he had arrived at Chester, and the north had been abandoned.

As day broke on 3 July the Allied army remained in possession of the field, which must have been a terrible site to behold, as Simeon Ashe writes:

> That night we kept the field, when the bodies of the dead were stripped. In the morning there was a mortifying object to behold, when the naked bodies of thousands lay upon the ground, and many not altogether dead.

After spending the day close to the battlefield, reorganising, tending to their wounded, and arranging for the burial of the dead by the local villagers, the Allied forces were much relieved by the arrival of Sir John Meldrum and Sir William Brereton, with a large force of Cheshire and Lancashire troops. It is not recorded when the Earl of Leven and Lord Fairfax returned to the army, but it must have been with some embarrassment that the pair slipped back into camp! The arrival of the reinforcements prompted the Allied commanders to return to their siege lines around York, and a Royalist correspondent, a Mr Ogden, reported their arrival:

> When the enemy heard that the Prince was gone they face York again on Thursday [4th], though far off upon a hill; and York salutes them with 3 pieces of ordnance, which they never heard before. They summoned the city to yield within 6 hours, but they set them at defiance and Sir Thomas Glemham sent the Prince word that he would keep it to the last man.

Sandal Castle – looking through the outer walls towards the keep.

As well as recommencing the siege of York, the Allies also sent a large force to intercept Prince Rupert, although, other than a couple of small clashes in Lancashire, this force was unable to stop the Prince's march into Cheshire, as has already been mentioned.

The story of the second siege of York is quickly told. The defenders were in no condition to hold the city for a lengthy period of time, and Sir Henry Slingsby tells of the state of affairs after Newcastle and Rupert had departed:

> Thus were we left at York, out of all hope of relief, the town much distracted, and every one ready to abandon her; and to encourage them that were left in the town, and to get them to stay, they were fain to give out false reports, that the Prince had fallen upon the enemy suddenly and routed them, and that he was coming back again to the town; yet many left us, not liking to abide another siege; which after began.

The survivors of Marston Moor that remained in the city were formed into several ad hoc regiments to aid in quartering them, but they were in no fit state to undergo

The inner barbican and keep.

another siege and desertions were rife.

The Allies continued their preparations, raising several new batteries, building a bridge of boats across the River Fosse, and constructing numerous ladders to aid their troops when the assault began. Simeon Ashe reported that the Allied commanders were intent on storming the town if the defenders did not surrender. By 11 July it had become apparent to the defenders that the assault was imminent, and the Royalist commanders requested a parley. Simeon Ashe details the ensuing negotiations:

> Hereupon a treaty being desired by the enemy, Sir William Constable and Colonel Lambert, were sent by Lord Fairfax into the city, upon hostages sent out for their security and safe return. They went in on Saturday morning, and having spent that day in parley, they returned with this request to the three Generals, that there might be commissioners authorised, to treat and conclude upon Articles for the peaceable surrender of the city. Our three Generals having demanded the judgement of some Ministers, whether the work of the treaty, might be approved on the Lord's day, and receiving encouragement, they appointed the Lord Humby, Sir William Constable, and Colonel Montague, to go the next day into the town, three hostages being sent out of the town for their security. They continued their debate till Monday, about noon they returned, with Articles to be subscribed by the Generals.

The articles allowed the garrison to march from the city with the honours of war, and proceed to the nearest Royalist garrison at a speed of no more than ten miles per day. Any sick or wounded soldiers would be allowed to remain in the city until they were well enough to leave. One of the most interesting of the articles is that at least two-thirds of the garrison would be made up of Lord Fairfax's Yorkshiremen. The articles were granted by the Allied commanders, and it was agreed that the garrison should march out on Tuesday 16 July.

At eleven o'clock on the morning of 16 July 1644, the Royalist garrison began its march out of Micklegate Bar. The Allied army lined the road for a mile from the gate, and officers patrolled the line to ensure that no looting took place. Simeon Ashe reports the pitiful state of the garrison as it left the city:

> The fourth part of them, at least, who marched out of the town were women, many very poor in their apparel, and others in better fashion. Most of the men had filled, and distempered themselves with drink; the number of the soldiers, as we conjectured, was not above a thousand, besides the sick and wounded persons.

Once the garrison had left the city, the Allied generals, and many of their officers, attended a service in the Minster, where Robert Douglas, the Earl of Leven's chaplain, gave praise 'unto God'. The city was in a terrible state, and Simeon Ashe estimated that it would cost £100,000 to repair the damage caused during the siege. The care of the city was given over to Lord Fairfax and his army, and a plaque in the Chapter House at York Minster still commemorates his good ministrations.

The Royalist troops continued their march as far as Hessay, where they camped for the night. Many of them were local men, and it must have been with some foreboding that they realised that they would not be seeing their homes for some time. Sir Henry Slingsby, a local man, sums up his feelings:

> Upon these articles we march out, but find a failing in the performance at the very first, for the soldier was pillaged, our wagons plundered, mine the first day, and others the next. Thus disconsolate we march, forced to leave our country, unless we would apostate, not daring to see mine own house, nor take a farewell of my children, although we lay the first night at Hessay within 2 miles of my house.

It must have been with heavy hearts that the local men continued their march. Slingsby is not the only person to mention the plundering of the Royalist soldiers as they marched, completely against the articles of surrender, and Simeon Ashe supports his story, writing at length about the 'wrongs' committed by the Allied soldiery. The Earl of Manchester ordered Oliver Cromwell, and a number of other officers, to investigate these accusations, and these enquiries were still in progress when the three Allied armies separated.

By 22 July the three Allied armies had gone their separate ways, prompted by the lack of supplies around York. Initially, the Scots moved into the West Riding, around Leeds and Wakefield, but by the 30th a decision had been made to march north to join the Earl of Callendar's Scottish army at Newcastle. The Earl of Manchester had decided to take his army back into the Eastern Association, where it could increase its strength and re-equip its tired regiments. Manchester would march his men south at a very leisurely pace, much to the chagrin of Oliver Cromwell, his Lieutenant-General. Reaching Doncaster on 23 July, Manchester despatched a small force to summon Tickhill Castle, which surrendered on the 26th. He then continued south, summoning, and receiving, the surrender of Sheffield Castle and Newcastle's house at Welbeck.

By the end of August 1644 Lord Fairfax was once again in sole command of the Parliamentary forces within Yorkshire. His task remained the reduction of a number of fortified locations: Skipton Castle, Knaresborough Castle, Sandal Castle, Pontefract Castle, Helmsley Castle, Scarborough Castle and Bolton Castle, and their small satellite garrisons. No Royalist field army remained within the county, or in any of the northern counties. The only surviving remnant of Newcastle's once mighty army was the Northern Horse, which had marched south with Rupert, and would remain campaigning in the south for some considerable time, although some elements, for example Sir John Mayney's brigade of horse, fought in the Furness area.

Sir John had been tasked with relieving Carlisle Castle, besieged by the Scots, but was unable to do so. Thinking on his feet he decide to drive the 1,000 head of cattle he had gathered over the Pennines to Skipton, and then on to Pontefract Castle. Setting off on 10 September, and marching at night, he arrived safely at Skipton with the loss of only one man during a brief skirmish at Ingleton. Leaving some of the cattle with Colonel Mallory, the commander of the Skipton garrison, he continued on to Pontefract, having surprised and defeated a newly-raised troop of Parliamentary horse near Bradford. He then inflicted a defeat on the Parliamentary force besieging Pontefract Castle, before delivering the remainder of the cattle to the garrison and continuing on to join the garrison at Newark. This must rate as one of the most outstanding cavalry feats of the entire war.

The war in Yorkshire degenerated into a series of sieges, raids, and counter-raids. On 4 November a relief force was despatched from Skipton and Knaresborough to relieve the beleaguered garrison at Helmsley Castle. Initially successful, the Royalist force was counterattacked by the Parliamentarian besieging force and driven off. With little chance of relief, Helmsley Castle surrendered several days later. The next step in the reduction of the remaining Royalist garrisons was to lay siege to Knaresborough, which capitulated on 20 December 1644.

By the end of the year only five major garrisons still held out for the King. Pontefract was already under siege, and the siege of Scarborough would begin in January 1645. The other three garrisons were blockaded. Further south, the King, who had had a successful year's campaigning, laid his plans for the coming year. Sir Marmaduke Langdale, and the other officers of the Northern Horse, urged him to march into Yorkshire, where the Parliamentary forces were weak. Once the county was recovered it would prove to be a fruitful recruiting ground. The King refused to march north, but gave Langdale permission to carry out a brief foray into the county to relieve Pontefract Castle.

On 23 February Langdale and his men, numbering about 1,500, left Banbury and marched towards Daventry. By the 26th they were a few miles north of Newark, where, on the 27th, they were reinforced by 400 horse and 400 foot from the Newark garrison. The night of 28 February was spent at Doncaster, and early on 1 March the Royalists set off on their approach march to Pontefract. Sir Gamaliel Dudley, who was with the Northern Horse, writes:

> We marched without sight of enemy, till we came near Wentbridge, above three miles short of Pontefract, where about 1,000 horse, and 500 dragoons of the enemy's, attended that place, as much as possibly they could to impede the speed of our course that way; but without much danger in the dispute, we forced the pass, but yet they so retarded our march, as the besiegers had gained time to be all drawn together both horse and foot in order, being in number about 2,500 foot and near 4,000 horse and dragoons, all the strength of the English that possibly the Lord Fairfax could draw together in the north, excepting the forces that Meldrum lay withal before Scarborough and Sir John Saville before Sandal, with which he (the Lord Fairfax) himself in person came this morning unto them, with two regiments of horse and 500 commanded musketeers.

Between four and five in the afternoon, the Royalists reached a hill overlooking the castle, with the Parliamentary forces formed at its foot. Having advanced in order of battle, Langdale ordered his men to engage, and Dudley gives some details of the ensuing fight:

> The fight continued without a clear victory, at the least three hours, until there was not left of our party, standing in order to charge withal, more than three final bodies, consisting of above 120 in each body, which with some officers and gentlemen together rallied, gave a seasonable charge to the last of the enemy's strength, the Castle at the same instant making a

Scarborough, looking along the front towards the castle.

gallant sally of 200 musketeers, who fell in the rear of the enemy's foot, our own foot firing upon them at the same time in their flank, and this totally cleared the field. We followed the execution six or seven miles, three several ways, as the enemy fled.

Dudley reports 300 enemy killed on the field, with many more drowned in the pursuit. The Royalists had taken between 700 and 800 prisoners, twenty-two colours of foot, and twenty-six standards of horse, and a large quantity of arms and ammunition. Royalist losses had been negligible, and Pontefract Castle had been relieved. Langdale used the following day to gather supplies for the garrison throughout the local countryside. Once the garrison was supplied, and following the King's orders, Langdale marched south again, arriving at Newark on 4 March. The Northern Horse's foray into Yorkshire had given Pontefract Castle a breathing space, but the Parliamentarians soon returned to take up the siege again.

Lord Fairfax's slow but steady campaign of reducing the remaining Royalist fortresses continued with sieges at Pontefract and Scarborough, while Skipton, Bolton and Sandal castles all continued to be blockaded. On 14 June the King's army, including the Northern Horse, was decisively defeated at Naseby by Parliament's New Model Army, commanded by Sir Thomas Fairfax, with Oliver Cromwell as his Lieutenant-General. Once again Cromwell's troopers proved the decisive element of the army, and virtually the whole of the King's veteran infantry was destroyed, although most of his horse managed to escape. The Royalist cause was in shambles, and the remainder of the 1st Civil War became an extended mopping-up operation.

In Yorkshire, following the battle of Naseby, both Pontefract and Scarborough castles capitulated within a few days, Pontefract on 20 July and Scarborough on the 25th. Sandal Castle in turn fell on 1 October, leaving only Bolton and Skipton castles remaining. The Parliamentary forces were closing in, and events in Yorkshire were mirrored across the nation. Skipton had undergone a short siege in early August, but the Parliamentary force had been withdrawn to oppose a possible incursion into South Yorkshire by the King and the remnants of his army. The King's meanderings through the Midlands eventually brought him to Chester,

St Mary's Church, which was part-ruined during the siege of Scarborough Castle.

where his army was defeated at Rowton Heath on 24 September, while Charles watched the action from a tower on the city walls.

Only in Scotland was the Royalist cause having some success, where the Marquis of Montrose, with a small force of Irish and Highlanders, was leading the Covenanters a merry chase. A decision was made to despatch the remnants of the Northern Horse to reinforce the Marquis, under the command of Lord Digby. Digby had recently been appointed as the King's Lieutenant-General of the Northern Counties, and had last been seen in Yorkshire in early 1642, when he plotted with Sir John Hotham to hand Hull, and its magazine, over to the King.

Digby's force consisted of about 1,200 men, made up of two brigades of the Northern Horse, commanded by Sir Marmaduke Langdale, with Sir Philip Monkton and Sir William Blakiston as his brigade commanders. Elements of other regiments, including Digby's own, may also have been present. The force left Worksop on 14 October, passing through Doncaster during the early evening, and raiding a number of Parliamentary quarters during the night. On the 15th Digby's men continued north, crossing the River Aire at Ferrybridge, and continuing towards Sherburn-in-Elmet. A captured messenger informed Digby and Langdale that the garrison at Sherburn was not aware of their approach, and the two decided to attack the village. The garrison was found forming on a moor about half a mile to the north of the town. When they spotted the Royalist horse approaching, the whole body, some 1,200–1,300 strong, fell into disorder and ran to a nearby wood, closely pursued by the Royalist horse. Two troops of Parliamentary horse appeared

Scarborough Castle – main gate.

Scarborough Castle keep, which was destroyed during the siege.

Scarborough Castle keep.

Pontefract: the ruined church between the castle and Baghill. This was part of the castle's outer defences.

on the scene, and these too were sent packing. For two men wounded, one of whom was Blakiston, the Royalists had captured 7–800 men, complete with their arms, ammunition and colours.

As the Royalists gathered their prisoners and counted their gains, a large force of Parliamentary horse was approaching Sherburn from the south. Early in the morning the regiments of Colonels Copley, Alured Lillburne and Lord Fairfax

Pontefract Castle, main keep.

rendezvoused at Brampton, between Rotherham and Barnsley. Following in the wake of the Northern Horse, their commander, Colonel Copley, despatched messages to Pontefract and Ferrybridge to warn the troops there of the Royalist presence, and another to York to request Lambert and Wren's regiments of horse to reinforce them.

The Parliamentary horse got to within half a mile of Sherburn before they were spotted, when the Royalist scouts reported a body of 500 horse advancing towards them from the direction of South Milford, to the south of Sherburn. Langdale led a small body of horse to oppose them, which was quickly reinforced by Langdale's own regiment. It was at this time that the remainder of Copley's force hoved into view, and Langdale called for Digby to bring up the rest of the Royalist horse.

In due course the two forces formed up in the fields astride the Sherburn–South Milford road. The Royalists numbered about 1,000 men, while the Parliamentary troops totalled between 1,300 and 1,400.

The action was over very quickly. At first the Royalists made good progress against the Parliamentary centre, but they in turn were routed by the Parliamentary reserves. The Parliamentary forces pursued the fleeing Royalists through the streets of Sherburn, taking many prisoners, before Colonel Copley reformed them on the north side of the village.

Digby and Langdale gathered the shattered remnants of their force, possibly as few as 600 men, and continued their march to Skipton, where they were reinforced by 100 men from the garrison. Continuing across the Pennines and through Cumberland into southern Scotland, stunning news reached them. Montrose had been defeated at the battle of Philiphaugh on 13 September by David Leslie, who had commanded the Scots horse in support of Cromwell at Marston Moor. Montrose's army had been destroyed, and the Marquis was on the run. To make matters worse several Parliamentary and Scottish forces were closing in on them, and in a short action at Burgh-on-Sands, near to Carlisle, on 20 October, the last of the Northern Horse were scattered, their leaders escaping by boat to the Isle of Man.

The last remnants of Newcastle's once victorious army had been destroyed. In Yorkshire only the garrisons of Skipton Castle and Bolton Castle still held out, and it was to these last two remaining Royalist outposts that Lord Fairfax now turned his attention. Reduced to eating horseflesh, the defenders of Bolton Castle capitulated on 6 November. Skipton lasted for another six weeks, when, with no hope of relief, the garrison surrendered on 21 December. Sir John Mallory, and his men, marched out of the castle with colours flying and drums sounding, but their capitulation meant that the King had no garrison remaining north of the River Trent, and all the northern counties had been brought under Parliament's sway. The 1st Civil War continued for another 12 months, with Parliament bringing more and more of the country under its control as the months passed. On 30 January 1647 King Charles surrendered to the Scots at Newark. Exactly one year later he was executed at Whitehall, and England became a Commonwealth for the next eleven years, until the Restoration of Charles II in 1660.

When King Charles had written to Prince Rupert in the summer of 1644, his letter said 'If York be lost I shall esteem my crown little else'. How prophetic had this statement been? Yorkshire, and the counties to its north, County Durham and

Skipton Castle, main gate.

Skipton Castle, main keep.

Skipton Castle, rear view.

Northumberland, had always proved to be fruitful recruiting grounds for the King's cause, as is shown by the number of northern regiments that marched south with him in July 1642. In 1643 the Royalist cause had reached its zenith, but even at it highest point a dark cloud appeared on the horizon. Newcastle's victory at Adwalton Moor forced Parliament's hand in coming to an agreement with the Scots, which led to a large Scots army entering northern England in 1644. Rupert's defeat at Marston Moor had several repercussions. First, one of the King's field armies had, to all intents and purposes, been destroyed. Second, Parliament no longer considered Prince Rupert an invincible commander. Third, two officers, Sir Thomas Fairfax and Oliver Cromwell, came to the fore, and when Parliament raised its New Model Army in early 1645, the pair were promoted to General and Lieutenant-General respectively. They proved to be a war-winning team, and built the New Model Army into a force which would become the direct parent of the modern British Army. Finally, in the aftermath of Marston Moor, the Royalists lost control of the whole of the north, with the exception of a few scattered garrisons. Parliament was able to concentrate its armies in the south to combat the King's Oxford army, and what followed was inevitable.

When York fell on 16 July 1644, the King's crown was indeed lost, and his fortunes went into a steady decline. When he wrote those prophetic words to his nephew he could not have known that not only would he lose his crown, but also his head to the executioner's axe on a cold January day in Whitehall.

BATTLEFIELD WALKS

Introduction

Having looked at the events of the 1st Civil War in Yorkshire, it is now time to cover the ground. The following section provides a number of battlefield walks to allow you to visit the sites of these actions. Many of the battles covered in the book were fought in a fairly confined area and the associated walks are, therefore, quite short. Although some historical information is given in the walks, this should be used in conjunction with the relevant chapters to provide a full picture of the battle.

The battle of Seacroft Moor does not have a battlefield walk provided. This is for two reasons. The first is the size of the battlefield. From the first contact above Bramham village to the final charge close to Seacroft is about seven miles, with little action between the two points. The area of the final fight is difficult to determine exactly, and the whole area is heavily built over. Local tradition has it that the final fight took place close to the A64 as it approaches Seacroft from the direction of York. As the road approaches Seacroft it joins with the main Leeds ring road, at a large roundabout. A couple of hundred yards before this roundabout a public house stands on the right-hand side of the road: the Old Red Lion. It is said that it is in this area that Sir Thomas Fairfax's men made their short stand, before they were overrun by George Goring's horsemen.

W A L K   O N E
The Battle of Tadcaster
6 December 1642

❶ Heading into Tadcaster from east, or west, along the A64, turn into Chapel Street and then right into the car park, which at the time of writing is free. Public conveniences are also available in the car park.

❷ Proceed from the car park onto the High Street. Looking west you can see the breweries that Tadcaster is famous for. Looking east you can see the bridge and York Road rising towards the crest of the hill. On the day of the battle the High Street would have been packed with Parliamentary troops, initially preparing to withdraw to the west, and later acting as reinforcements for the fighting over on the east bank.

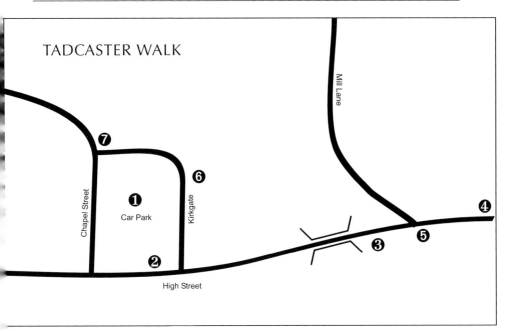

TADCASTER WALK

❸ Carry on as far as the bridge. In 1642 part of the roadway was broken down to prevent access into the town across the bridge. The gap was covered with planks to allow the Parliamentary troops to cross. Looking south down the River Wharfe it becomes clear why the Duchess of Newcastle thought the river unfordable except at the bridge, particularly during winter – the Wharfe is still susceptible to flooding today. Looking north a viaduct can be seen in the distance. Just to the south is a weir, and this is close to the spot where a mill stood on the east bank.

❹ Continue over the bridge and along York Road, taking note of the entrance to Mill Lane on your left – we will come back to this later. Carry on to the brow of the hill, where the road begins to sweep right and descend. Although the area is now built over this is almost certainly where Lord Fairfax raised his earthwork, probably on the north side of the road. It can be seen from the lack of level ground that it is not very likely that Fairfax was able to build a large and strong fort as described by the Duchess of Newcastle. It is much more likely that the defences took the form of a number of breastworks, possibly incorporating some of the houses that stood on the site, and their enclosures. Newcastle's men attacked from the north and east and were driven back to shelter among the hedges that stood close by. Looking back towards the town it can easily be seen why Fairfax wanted to prevent Newcastle from positioning guns in this area, as it overlooks the bridge and town.

In the area of the earthwork looking back towards the bridge.

❺ Return towards the bridge. When you reach Mill Lane, pause for a moment. Looking into Mill Lane you now look into a supermarket car park. At the time of the battle the lane continued north until it reached the riverbank, and then continued to the mill. Several buildings existed around this junction, and it is very likely these were the ones seized by the Royalists. It took a resolute attack to drive them out, when they would have continued their retreat towards the mill.

❻ Cross the bridge back onto the High Street. Turn right into Kirkgate, which contains two surviving contemporary buildings. Firstly, on the left-hand side, is 'The Ark', which was called Morley Hall at the time of the battle, and is now Tadcaster Council offices. At the end of Kirkgate stands St Mary's Church. The original church on the site was destroyed by the Scots in 1319, during one of their incursions in the aftermath of the Battle of Bannockburn.

❼ Continue along Kirkgate and turn into Chapel Street. The road continuing from this junction out of Tadcaster is the road from Wetherby. It is along this road that the Earl of Newport should have approached. Unfortunately for the Royalists this road remained annoyingly empty throughout the day of the battle. Carry on down Chapel Street and return to the car park. Two other walks in this book are within a short drive – Marston Moor and the King's Manor at York.

Looking down Mill Lane. Royalist troops captured the buildings around this junction, but were driven out by the defenders, and the buildings were set on fire.

The Storming of Leeds
23 January 1643

❶ Start your walk at the junction of the Headrow and Briggate, looking down Briggate. If you turn to your right you are looking up the Headrow, known at the time of the battle as the Upper Headrow. Walk to the crest of the hill, where the town hall and library should come into view. It was along this road that Sir Thomas Fairfax and his main force approached Leeds from Bradford. The road was barricaded at this point, and to either side was a 'trench', which in reality was a ditch and palisade, the defensive earthwork being as high as a man. The whole town, except the side bordering the River Aire, was surrounded by a similar defensive work. While Sir Thomas tried to force an entry at this point, he despatched two other forces, one north and one south. Sergeant-Major Forbes

Briggate looking towards the Headrow. Parliamentary forces advanced up the hill towards the old Market Place.

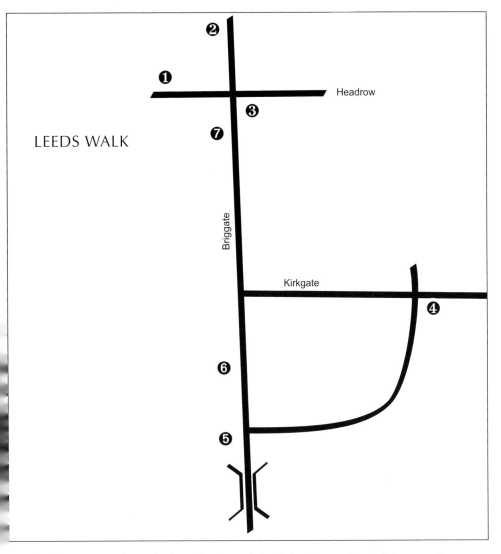

LEEDS WALK

Headrow

Briggate

Kirkgate

led his men southwards along the line of the defensive works until he was close to the river, while Sir William Fairfax and his men moved north around the works.

❷ Walk back up the Headrow until you reach Briggate and then turn left. On your left-hand side is St John's Church, identified in contemporary accounts as the New Kirk. The church stood inside the defensive works, and it was in this area that Sir William Fairfax attacked the defences.

❸ Return to the junction of the Headrow and Briggate, then cross the road into the top of Briggate. Looking down the street today you have a very different view from that at the time of the battle. Today the view is usually blocked by the

Briggate looking towards the old Market Place.

shoppers thronging the street, but at the time of the battle several buildings stood in the middle of the street. The top section of modern Briggate was originally known as the Market Place. Below this was a short row of buildings, which at one time were butchers' shops, hence the name of the row – Shambles. Next was the town hall, again sitting in the centre of Briggate.

❹   Walk down Briggate until you reach Debenhams, and turn left into Kirkgate. Walk down Kirkgate until you reach the Market Hall, which should be on your left. At the bottom of Kirkgate stands the Old Kirk, as it is referred to in the contemporary accounts.

❺   From the market follow the road around past the Corn Exchange. Bearing right, you will come to the bottom of Briggate. Turn left, pass under the railway bridge, and before you is the bridge over the River Aire: not the original one, but in the same position. Over the bridge another Parliamentary force, commanded by Captain Mildmay, approached the town from the direction of Hunslet. This force cleared the enemy positions on the south bank of the Aire, and helped Forbes's men to break into the town. It is close to where you are standing that Mr Schofield led his men in singing Psalm 68, as they climbed into the enemy defensive works. Further up Briggate another, larger, enemy work was taken, as the Parliamentarians continued their push up the street.

❻   Walk back up Briggate until you reach Marks and Spencer. Contemporary accounts talk of a demi-culverin being positioned in the street, and it must have been somewhere close to this spot, as the town hall stood only slightly further up the street. Mr Schofield, a preacher, led an attack on this gun and captured it, killing the crew in the process.

❼   Following in the Parliamentarian footsteps, continue to the top of Briggate. As Forbes and Mildmay's men drove the enemy back up Briggate, Sir Thomas Fairfax was able to clear the barricade from across the Headrow, and lead several troops of horse in a charge up the street. The two forces met at the top of Briggate, in what was then the Market Place. The Royalist forces had been routed, and their commander, Sir William Saville, had almost been drowned trying to escape by swimming the Aire, along with many of his men. The remainder were taken prisoner.

The Storming of Wakefield

Wakefield has changed considerably over the years, and its street plan differs from that at the time of the battle, unlike Leeds, Tadcaster and Selby, where the main streets still follow the lines they did at the time of the Civil Wars. That aside, sections of Wakefield's original four streets still exist in places, and the cathedral forms a central point for a short walk.

❶ Start your walk at the cathedral, outside the entrance to the shopping mall. Looking up the hill you can see the remnants of the Market Place. Walk down the hill into Warrengate, and continue to its end. At the time of the storming Warrengate was the main route into Wakefield from the east, but now it ends at the dual carriageway that by-passes the town centre to the east. Close to this point a barricade stood, where Major-General Gifford and Sir Thomas Fairfax attacked the town. Gifford's foot cleared the barricade, allowing Sir Thomas Fairfax's horse to enter the town. A body of Royalist horse commanded by Colonel George Goring, who reeled in his saddle as he led the charge, counterattacked them. It is said that he had risen from his sick bed, but local tradition has it that he had attended a bowling party at a local hall, along with many of the officers of the garrison, and was still half drunk! The Royalist horse were driven back, and Goring was captured. He spent the next year in captivity, most of it in the Tower of London, until he was exchanged in the summer of 1644.

❷ Returning towards the cathedral, stop at the bottom end of the close. Near to this spot Sir Thomas Fairfax found himself cut off from his men, and had to jump his horse over a barricade to escape.

❸ Continue to the top end of the cathedral. Major-General Gifford led his men along Warrengate, along with a captured cannon. In the Market Place a large body of Royalist foot was formed up. Gifford planted the cannon in the churchyard, and summoned the Royalists to surrender. When they refused he ordered the gun to open fire. The Royalists began to waver, and a charge by Fairfax's horse finished the job, causing the bulk of the garrison to surrender. Fairfax and his 1,500 men had stormed a town garrisoned by twice their number, capturing most of the enemy in the process.

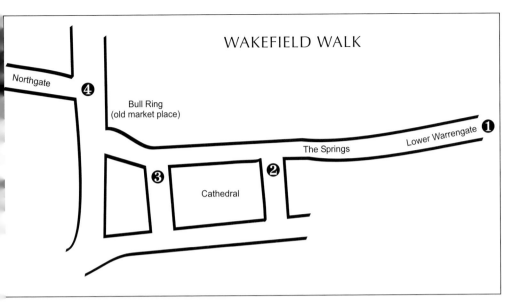

WAKEFIELD WALK

Northgate

Bull Ring
(old market place)

The Springs

Lower Warrengate

Cathedral

④ Continue through the Market Place and into Northgate. Another Parliamentary column, commanded by Sir Henry Foulis and Sir William Fairfax, assaulted the barricade at the end of this street. It is not known whether their attack was successful, as contemporary accounts speak of the attack along Warrengate as the decisive one.

Two other places close to the town centre are worth visiting:

The first is the chapel on the bridge. This is down Kirkgate, just off the main road out of Wakefield to Barnsley and Doncaster. Shakespeare has this as the site of the slaying of Edmund, Earl of Rutland, son of Richard, Duke of York, by Lord Clifford, in the rout after the Battle of Wakefield in 1460, early in the Wars of the Roses. Local tradition, however, has the slaying further up Kirkgate, towards the town. The chapel contained the town records, and was pillaged by Fairfax's men after the storming.

Continuing out of Wakefield on the A61 towards Barnsley you will see signs for Sandal Castle, having driven through the Wars of the Roses battlefield on the A61. Sandal Castle was the scene of a prolonged siege during the 1st Civil War, and the traces of its defensive earthworks can still be seen.

The Battle of Adwalton Moor

❶ A good starting point for your walk is Drighlington Library. Here you are standing in the centre of Adwalton Moor, close to the scene of much of the action in the battle. Walk from the car park to the front door of the library, where an information board is displayed. This board, and four stones placed on the battlefield, were raised in 2000 by Leeds Council, Morley Rotary Club, Groundwork, the English Civil War Society, and the Yorkshire Battlefield Society, and funded by local businesses. Walking back to the car park, the first of the stones can be seen.

❷ At the entrance to the car park turn left and proceed down Moorland Road, continuing past the first junction until you come to its junction with Whitehall Road. Then turn left along Whitehall Road until you arrive at the roundabout. Follow the A650 towards Bradford for a few yards and then cross the road and follow the track up onto the old railway embankment. Find a position from which you can see along the A650 towards Bradford. The hill in front of you is known locally as Whiskett, or Westgate Hill, and it is across its slopes that the initial part of the battle was fought. Looking across the A650 you can see a number of houses in the distance, and these mark the line of the old A650. This was the old road from Wakefield to Bradford, and it was along this road that both armies marched on the morning of the battle: the Royalists towards Bradford, and the Parliamentary army towards Howley Hall, in the direction of Wakefield. Half a mile beyond the nearest ridge of Whiskett Hill the advance guards of the two armies collided. The Royalists were driven back to the ridge, and, once reinforced, made a stand. In the meantime the remainder of the Royalist army was deploying on to Adwalton Moor, just beyond the library. The Parliamentary army then drove the Royalist musketeers from the ridge, through a number of enclosures to the edge of the moor, marked by a field boundary opposite where you are standing, which joins onto Whitehall Road close to its junction with Moorland Road. While this was happening, the main body of the Parliamentary army deployed along the ridge in front of you and prepared to advance.

❸ Retrace your steps onto Whitehall Road and proceed for several hundred yards until you come to the Malt Shovel public house. You have a good view of the line of the Parliamentary advance down the hill from the pub's car park. The

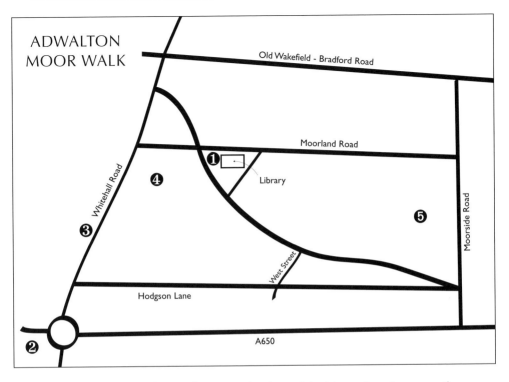

hedge line across in front of you marks the original boundary between the enclosures, above the line, and the moor, below the line and to your rear. The Royalist musketeers lined the hedge, and the Parliamentary army marched down the hill to engage them, driving them from their positions back onto the moor.

❹ Return to Whitehall Road and turn left, crossing to the other side of the road when you get chance. Follow the buildings around to the right until you are standing looking back towards the library and Hungar Hill beyond. The main Royalist army was deployed on the lower slopes of Hungar Hill, above the library, and stretched from the road to your left, Hodgson Lane, to the old A650 and possibly beyond, with horse on either flank and pike and guns in the centre. The infantry regiments had been split in two, with the musketeers advancing to engage the Parliamentary army among the enclosures, while the pike stood in blocks, waiting to advance. To your right, where the buildings now stand, was an area of enclosures, which were occupied by Sir Thomas Fairfax's men. These were attacked on two occasions by large bodies of Royalist horse, but held their ground, driving the enemy back towards their guns.

❺ Cross the moor until you are on the hill above the library, close to Moorside Road, and turn back to face the library. You are now standing at approximately the position of the Royalist army. Below you the Royalist musketeers had been driven back onto the moor, and their Parliamentary opponents had begun to advance. Looking half left, towards the building to the left of your last position, you would have seen a large body of Royalist horse being driven back up the hill towards your present location, pursued by a much smaller body of Parliamentary horse, led by Sir Thomas Fairfax. At this stage of the battle the Royalists were on the verge of defeat, and the Earl of Newcastle had issued orders to withdraw. It was at this point that one of his officers, Colonel Posthumous Kirton, led a body of pikemen forward to attack the advancing Parliamentary forces. This was the turning point of the battle. As more Royalist troops joined Kirton's attack, the Parliamentary advance was first halted and then driven back. Within a short time the whole Parliamentary left wing was in flight back towards Bradford, over Whiskett Hill and along the old road. Sir Thomas Fairfax and his men had withdrawn into the enclosures they had occupied, and held their ground until an order to withdraw reached Fairfax from his father. He successfully disengaged, but was unable to return to Bradford, marching to Halifax instead, before rejoining his father in Bradford that night.

There are two other places close to the battlefield that are worth a visit: Oakwell Hall and Bolling Hall.

Oakwell Hall, front view.

Oakwell Hall, rear view.

Oakwell Hall

To get to Oakwell Hall drive back along the modern A650 towards Wakefield. After several hundred yards you will see a sign for Birstall. Turn right and follow the road down into Birstall, where you will see signs for Oakwell Hall. The hall is a pretty early Jacobean house, owned by the Batt family at the time of the battle. One of the family members was Captain John Batt, one of the Earl of Newcastle's officers, although it is not known whether he served at Adwalton Moor.

Oakwell Hall. John Batt, the owner of the hall at the time of the battle, served in Newcastle's army.

Bolling Hall

Follow the A650 towards Bradford. As you approach the city Bolling Hall is clearly signposted. The Earl of Newcastle used Bolling Hall as his headquarters during the siege of Bradford, which followed the battle of Adwalton Moor. Local tradition has it that he was visited by a spirit during the night before the town was taken, which implored him to 'Pity poor Bradford'. The bedroom in which this visitation is supposed to have taken place is still decorated in the style it was during the Earl's stay. The hall also contains a number of artefacts from the battle, including cannonballs and a helmet.

Bolling Hall, front view.

Bolling Hall, rear view.

The Actions at Selby

Two actions took place within the streets of Selby. On 2 July 1643 a short, sharp, cavalry action took place during the Fairfaxes' retreat to Hull, in the aftermath of the battle of Adwalton Moor. The second action took place on 14 April 1644, when Lord Fairfax's Yorkshire Parliamentary forces stormed the town, just prior to the siege of York. Each action will be discussed in turn, although you may cover the same ground. A good starting point for both short walks is the Market Place, close to the Abbey.

2 July 1643

A Start in the Market Place, looking towards the abbey. To your left is Finkle Street, which then opens into Micklegate. It was in the Market Place that Sir Thomas Fairfax and his forty men waited for their Royalist pursuers.

B Walk into Finkle Street and look along Micklegate. At the far end of the street New Millgate enters into Micklegate from the left. This was the main road into Selby from the direction of Tadcaster and Cawood. It was along this road that

Selby Market Place looking towards Finkle Street. The Royalist Horse emerged from this narrow opening to be struck by Fairfax's awaiting troopers.

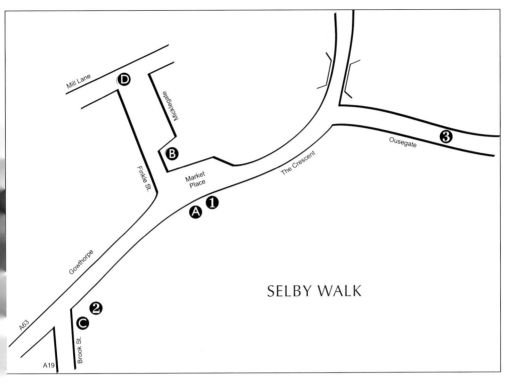

SELBY WALK

Lord Fairfax withdrew during the night after the battle of Tadcaster, and three troops of Royalist horse, from Cawood Castle, approached the town. Finding no opposition they continued along Micklegate and into Finkle Street. As they emerged into the Market Place their column was struck in the flank by Sir Thomas Fairfax's men, and split in two.

Ⓒ Turn right as you enter the Market Place and walk along Gowthorpe (A63) until you reach its junction with Brook Street (A19). At the time of the Civil Wars, Brook Street was known as Brayton Lane, and was, as it still is, the road to Doncaster. Half of the fleeing Royalist horse galloped down Gowthorpe and turned into Brayton Lane, pursued by a small number of Fairfax's men.

Ⓓ Return to Finkle Street and walk up Micklegate towards New Millgate. At the time of the battle, Millgate was so narrow that during the storming of Selby in 1644 it was not even defended. As the remainder of the Royalist horse fled along Micklegate, pursued by Fairfax and part of his force, a further body of Parliamentary horse entered the street from Millgate. Seeing the Royalist horse galloping down Micklegate, and not realising they were being pursued by Fairfax, the Parliamentary late arrivals turned and tried to flee into Millgate, where the

The Market Place and abbey. Finkle Street enters from the left.

whole mass of horse came to a halt. During the fight, before the Royalists managed to get clear and gallop all the way back to Cawood, Sir Thomas was wounded in the wrist by a pistol ball, having to dismount while his wound was dressed. This short, sharp fight ensured that Lord Fairfax, and his entourage, managed to cross the Ouse by ferry – no bridge existed at the time – and escape to Hull. Sir Thomas and his men continued south along the southern bank of the Humber, where they were picked up by ship at Barton on Humber, and ferried into Hull.

14 April 1644

❶ Start in the Market Place, facing the abbey. Turn left and walk to the entrance to Finkle Street. At the far end of Micklegate, Millgate exits the left-hand side of the street, and continues to Tadcaster and Cawood. Millgate was so narrow that John Belasyse, the Royalist commander, did not even bother to defend it.

❷ Turn left and continue down Gowthorpe to its junction with Brook Street, known as Brayton Lane at the time of the battle. Selby was almost surrounded by water obstacles, with the Ouse to the north and the Selby Mill Dam to the west. The eastern side of the town was protected by the abbey fishponds. The only part of the town not covered by water was the area between Gowthorpe and Brayton Lane, and Lord Fairfax had rectified this by digging a ditch between the two during his army's stay in the town during the early part of 1643. This meant that the only entrances to the town were the roads: Gowthorpe, Brayton Lane, and Ousegate, all of which were barricaded and defended. The barricades on Gowthorpe and Brayton Lane were attacked during the storming, but the Parliamentary troops do not seem to have made much progress until Sir Thomas Fairfax broke into the town on Ousegate, and it is there that we will now proceed.

❸ Continue back up Gowthorpe towards the abbey, and into the Crescent and New Street. Ousegate is on the right, just before the bridge over the Ouse is reached. Turn into Ousegate, and continue as far as the railway bridge. It was close to this point that Sir Thomas Fairfax assaulted the barricade, forcing an entrance into the town after a hard fight, although one Royalist account states that Fairfax gained entrance to the town due to the cowardice, or treachery of, one Captain Williams, who commanded the troops at the barricade. Turn back towards the town centre. Fairfax led his troopers down Ousegate, and Belasyse led his mounted reserve from the Market Place in a savage counter-attack. Fairfax was unhorsed, and found himself alone among the enemy as his men were driven back along Ousegate. Fortunately, they quickly rallied and came to his relief. The Royalist horse broke, leaving their commander wounded and in the possession of the enemy. The bulk of the Royalist infantry were captured, along with their arms and ammunition, while the horse escaped towards Cawood and Pontefract. Although it was a relatively small action, the storming of Selby led directly to the siege of York, and, in turn, to the battle of Marston Moor. It was the first step in Parliament's conquest of the north.

Looking along Millgate. The street was so narrow that it was not defended.

The Assault on the King's Manor

❶ Start your walk at York Minster. Walk down High Petergate until you reach Bootham Bar. It is worth entering the bar and looking through the firing slits down Bootham towards St Mary's Tower. From here the defenders could have seen the Eastern Association troops assaulting the breach at St Mary's Tower.

York Minster, side view.

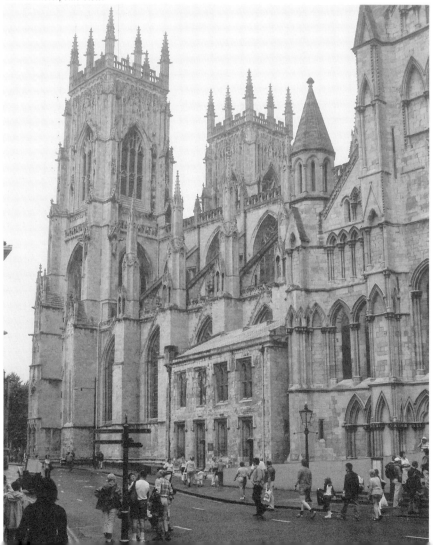

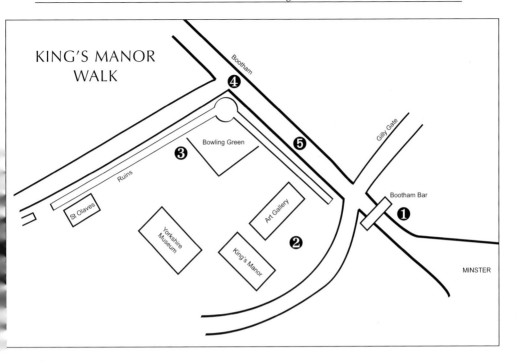

KING'S MANOR WALK

Bootham
Gilly Gate
Bowling Green
Ruins
St Olaves
Art Gallery
Yorkshire Museum
King's Manor
Bootham Bar
MINSTER

❷ Go through the gate into Bootham, and cross the road to the art gallery. To your left is the King's Manor House, which gave its name to the walled area around it. Follow the lane along the left-hand side of the manor, through into the park, and follow the path around to the right, which will bring you to the Yorkshire Museum. Beyond are the ruins of St Mary's Abbey, the work of Henry VIII and his Reformation of the church.

❸ Walk past the museum and head right, through the ruins, until you come to the wall of the bowling green, which was also a bowling green at the time of the assault. At the far side of the bowling green is St Mary's Tower, and it was here that Lawrence Crawford exploded the mine on the morning of 16 June. Little damage to the tower can be seen from here, but the wall to its left shows signs of a large breach, and it was not repaired to the same height as the original wall. Crawford's men stormed through the breach and into the bowling green, where they encountered a small force of defenders trying to block the gateway into the remainder of the King's Manor. This force was quickly overcome and the Parliamentarians continued further into the manor, to the area of the museum. Royalist reinforcements arrived quickly from the city, and halted the Parliamentary advance, while another force attempted to cut the attackers off from the breach.

High Petergate, from Bootham Bar.

❹ Walk back to the museum and follow the path past the ruins, and around to the right to St Olave's church, which was used as an observation post by the Royalists during the siege. Pass through the gate and turn right, up the hill. Continue until you reach the junction with Bootham, and St Mary's Tower. It can now clearly be seen what damage the mine caused. The whole of the front of the tower collapsed, along with a large section of wall to its right. It was through this breach that many of Crawford's men attacked, the remainder using ladders to climb the wall further down the hill. The Royalist counter-attack trapped many of the Parliamentary troops within the manor, and reinforcements could not reach

A musketeer's view, down Bootham from Bootham Bar.

them. A large number were killed, or surrendered. On the day after the assault the Parliamentary troops attempted to rescue the wounded and injured lying under and among the ruins of the tower, close to where you are standing, but were prevented from doing so by Royalist musket fire.

❺ Continue along Bootham, back towards the gate. On your right the walls show distinct marks, where houses were built against them, and chimneys and alcoves carved into the wall. These houses gave the Parliamentary forces cover to advance up the street, and it was Newcastle's error that these houses were not destroyed before the siege began, something he had done earlier in the year at Newcastle. The Royalists made several attempts to burn the houses down, but the vigilance of the Parliamentary troops prevented them from doing so.

Many other sites of interest are within the city walls, which provide a fascinating walk themselves. Two are of particular interest to the Civil War:

The first is Walmgate Bar, which still has a surviving barbican and shows the marks of the bombardment. It was outside this gate that Lord Fairfax raised a battery. A second mine had been dug to explode under the gate, but was prevented from doing so by flooding.

The second is the Castle Museum, which has a very good English Civil War exhibition.

Advancing to push of pike. Courtesy of John Wilson

The Battle of Marston Moor
2 July 1644

❶ Start at the obelisk, which lies on the road between Long Marston and Tockwith. Standing between the monument and the information board, with the monument behind you, you are looking towards the Royalist lines, and towards the main area of fighting. To your right is Long Marston, and to your left can be seen the roofs of Tockwith. The two villages marked the east and west extremities of the battlefield. Turning half right, you are looking across the fields towards where George Goring's cavalrymen were deployed in two lines. Turn back to face the information board, and then half left, to where you can see a large house set back in the fields. This is approximately the frontage covered by the Royalist foot, and beyond them was Byron's horse. Now turn to face the monument, and the ridge beyond. It was upon this ridge that the Allied army deployed during the afternoon of the battle. Sir Thomas Fairfax's horsemen were positioned on the western end of the ridge, in front of you to the left. Oliver Cromwell's men were stationed at the eastern end of the ridge, and the Allied foot were in between the two wings of horsemen. During the late afternoon the Allied army descended from the ridge and took up a line close to the road. At sometime between seven and seven-thirty in the evening the Allies moved forward to attack the Royalists, all along the line.

❷ Across the road from the monument a track leads up onto the ridge. Ascending the ridge will give you a much better view of the battlefield. To the right of the monument is Moor Lane, which leads into the centre of the battlefield. Several hundred yards beyond the road a hedge line can clearly be seen. This was the obstacle described in most contemporary accounts of the battle, which stretched from Long Marston to Tockwith, and covered the whole front of the Royalist army. It varied in composition from a hedge, to a ditch, or a combination of both, and although in some areas it formed a formidable obstacle, in other areas its effects were negligible. Between Sir Thomas Fairfax and George Goring the obstacle was particularly bad, as a six-foot bank had formed between the cultivated land and the moor beyond, down which Fairfax's horsemen had to descend.

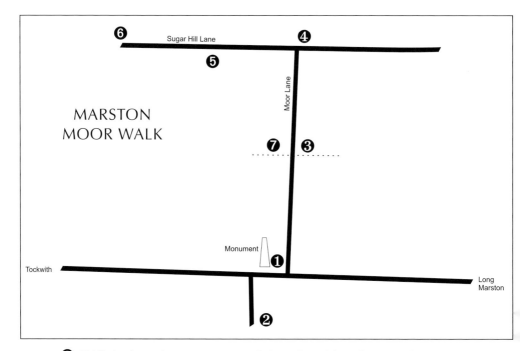

❸ Walk back to the monument, and then along Moor Lane until you come to the ditch, which was manned by Royalist musketeers as a forlorn hope. Beyond them the main body of the Royalist foot formed, supported by several bodies of horse. Look to your right, towards Long Marston. Across the fields to your front a large cavalry action was fought. The line of the obstacle continued from where you are standing towards Long Marston, and was formed by a high bank, down which Sir Thomas Fairfax's men had to descend, into the teeth of George Goring's commanded musketeers. A mass of musket balls has been recovered along this line. Disordered by their descent of the bank, and by the heavy musketry pounding them from the Royalist musketeers, Fairfax's horsemen were easy prey for Goring's counter-attack, and were driven in confusion back up the ridge. A second line of Royalist horse, commanded by Sir Charles Lucas, then swept towards where you are standing to strike the flank of the Allied foot. Turn around to look along the ditch towards Marston Grange. Close to where you are standing four regiments of Scots foot fought their way across the ditch. Beyond them a brigade of Lord Fairfax's had also fought their way over the obstacle, although they were quickly driven back by a fresh body of Royalist foot. Beyond them, close to Marston Grange, two brigades of the Earl of Manchester's foot advanced quickly, the obstacle in front of them being almost non-existent, and routed a detached brigade of Royalist foot, positioned to cover the gap in the obstacle.

❹ Continue along Moor Lane until you come to the junction at its end. This junction is called Four Lanes Meet. The track running across in front of you was used by the Marquess of Newcastle's foot, to reach the battlefield as it marched from York. Another track ran north, directly in front of you. This has now been ploughed away. The track running to the right is an extension of Moor Lane, and is known locally as Bloody Lane. Local children still dare one another to go up Bloody Lane after dark, such is its reputation!

❺ Turn left and walk down the lane that runs across the battlefield; Sugar Hill Lane. After a couple of hundred yards stop and look left towards the ridgeline. You are now behind the centre of the Royalist lines looking towards the ditch. In front of you is the area in which Lord Fairfax's foot crossed the ditch, and was driven back by a body of the Earl of Newcastle's foot. Then a brigade of Royalist horse struck Fairfax's disordered troops and routed them. Several regiments of Scottish foot also turned tail and fled, and the ridge in the distance would have been covered with fleeing Allied soldiers and pursuing Royalist horsemen. Looking half left to where the ditch meets Moor Lane (point 3 above), two regiments of Scots soldiers, Crawford-Lindsay and Maitland's, stood their ground against the continued charges of the Royalist left wing horse.

❻ Continue along Sugar Hill Lane until you come to its end, in a small field. This is White Syke Close, the traditional site of the last stand of Newcastle's Whitecoats. In front of you, over towards Tockwith, the Royalist right flank horse

The ditch looking towards the initial positions of Goring's horse. Sir Charles Lucas led the Royalist second line of horse in an attack on the Scots foot across the ground illustrated, towards the camera.

Four Lanes Meet looking towards York. Many Royalist troops tried to escape from the field along the lane in the centre. It is still known locally as 'Bloody Lane'.

were engaged and routed by Cromwell's Eastern Association Horse, supported by David Leslie's three regiments of Scots Horse. The fight was over quickly, and the remnants of the Royalist right wing fled past where you are standing towards Wilstrop Wood, the wooded area to your right. The Earl of Manchester's foot, approaching from the direction of Marston Grange and Cromwell's horse, approaching from your front, then fell upon the flank of the Royalist centre. It is at this point that a body of Newcastle's Whitecoats made a stand and fought virtually to the last man. Tradition has it that the Whitecoats fell, and were buried, in the area now covered by White Syke Close, although the close itself did not exist at the time of the battle. A recently published study of the artefacts found in a long-term survey of the battlefield shows little evidence to support this tradition. The only artefacts found in the area point to this being the route taken by the fleeing Royalist right wing horse. One modern author put forward a theory that the last stand took place in an enclosure on Atterwith Lane much further to the east, but the evidence for this is flimsy. The artefact evidence may suggest another area of the battlefield as the site of the Whitecoats' last stand, and it is to this point that we shall now return.

7 Retrace your steps along Sugar Hill Lane and Moor Lane until you come to the junction of the ditch and Moor Lane. The area on either side of the lane has revealed a mass of finds, particularly musket balls. The western side of Moor Lane has a massive concentration of finds in a fairly small area, where the ditch crosses the lane, and this area has recently been put forward as the site of the last stand. As well as the artefact evidence another couple of pieces of historical information may support this. The first is a map from the nineteenth century, which shows a wood in this area, called White Syke Whin – could this be how confusion has arisen about the location of the stand? The second is a newspaper article from 1859. Workmen were building an underground drain and dug into a massive grave pit, about four feet below the surface. They uncovered an area twelve yards long by eight wide and still hadn't got to the edge of the 'vast sepulchre'. Unfortunately, the article does not state exactly where the discovery took place, although an underground drain does pass through the area where you are standing, running east to west. The site of the gallant stand of the Whitecoats is still open to dispute, and will be until their grave pit is found. To the north of the ditch, at its junction with Moor Lane, is a pond, in exactly the position of White Syke Whin, and very close to the line of the drain. Could it be that the reason the grave pit has not come to light is that it now lies under water? For the time being, where the Whitecoats met their end must remain one of the mysteries of Marston Moor.

Gun and pike defend a position. Courtesy of John Wilson

Bibliography

Primary sources

A large number of contemporary and near contemporary accounts were used in the writing of this book, and quoted at length. It is beyond the scope of this work to produce an exhaustive list, but several of the main accounts are listed below:

Parsons, D. (Ed.), *The Diary of Sir Henry Slingsby*, 1836.

Firth, C.H. (Ed.), *Memoirs of the Duke of Newcastle*, 1886.

Bell, R., *Memorials of the Civil War, comprising the correspondence of the Fairfax Family with the most distinguished personages engaged in that memorable contest*, Vol. 1, 1849.

A Short Memoriall of the Northern Actions during Ye War there, from Ye yeare 1642 till 1644, Yorkshire Archaeological Journal, Vol. 8, 1884.

The two most useful accounts, which both cover the bulk of the actions covered in this book, are Newcastle's *Memoirs* and Sir Thomas Fairfax's *A Short Memoriall*. Both were written many years after the events by participants in the actions.

For those wanting to research further into the period many city libraries have extensive collections of Civil War material. The main libraries used by this author were York, York Minster, Leeds, Sheffield and Bradford. Hull and Beverley libraries also have extensive collections. Many local libraries have material pertinent to local events. For example, Selby and Tadcaster libraries both hold contemporary accounts of the actions fought within the streets of the towns.

Modern accounts

Below are listed some of the main accounts for the 1st Civil War in Yorkshire:

Cooke, D., *Adwalton Moor, The Forgotten Battle,* Battlefield Press, 1996.

Cooke, D., *Northern Thunder, The Battle of Marston Moor, 2nd July 1644,* Battlefield Press, 1997.

Johnson, D., *Adwalton Moor – The Battle that changed a war,* Blackthorn Press, 2003.

Newman, P.R., *The Battle of Marston Moor 1644,* Antony Bird, Chichester, 1981.

Newman, P.R. and P.R. Roberts, *Marston Moor 1644: The Battle of the Five Armies,* Blackthorn Press, 2003.

Wenham, P., *The Great and Close Siege of York, 1644,* York, 1994.

Young, P., *Marston Moor,* 1970.

The following two books give a good general account of the Civil Wars:

Young, P. and R. Holmes, *The English Civil War – A Military History of the Three Civil Wars 1642-1651,* PBS, 1974.

Reid, S. *All the King's Armies – A Military History of the English Civil War 1642-1651,* Spellmount, 1998.

Index

Adwalton, 66, 83
Adwalton Moor, 6, 8-9, 11, 13, 17, 19, 39, 45, 47, 61, 67, 69, 75, 79, 87, 92-94, 159
Adwalton Moor Walk, 170
Almonbury, 44
Alnwick, 96
Alured, Captain (later Colonel), 57-58, 156
Alured, Lieutenant, 58
Ashe, Simeon, 108-109, 111, 113-115, 118, 130, 132, 134, 136-138, 144, 148, 150-151
Baillie, Lieutenant-General, 132, 139
Banbury, 152
Barnsley, 53, 157
Barton, 91-92
Basset, Elizabeth, 19
Basset, William, 19
Batley, 55, 64
Baume, Isaac, 33
Beeston, 41
Belasyse, Colonel John, 97-99, 101, 103-106
Berwick-on-Tweed, 97
Bethell, Sir Hugh, 134
Beverley, 16, 18, 81
Bilton Bream, 124-125, 128, 139-140
Bingley, 31
Birkhead, Captain, 44
Blakiston, Sir William, 129, 137-138, 154, 156
Bolling Hall, 79, 82, 86
Bolsover, 19
Bolton, 47, 100, 118, 120
Bolton Castle, 148, 151, 153, 157
Boroughbridge, 11, 120
Bourchier, Elizabeth, 95
Bradford, 8, 13, 18, 29-31, 33-35, 37-39, 47, 53, 55, 64-69, 71, 73, 76-79, 81-84, 98-99, 139, 151
Bramham Moor, 21, 50-51
Brampton, 157
Brandling, Colonel, 97
Brayton, 88
Breda, 37
Brereton, Sir William, 148
Bridlington, 46-47
Bright, Captain John, 57-58
Bristol, 100-101
Burgh-on-Sands, 157
Bury, 118, 120
Byron, Sir John, 98, 117-118, 127-128, 132, 139-141
Byron, Sir Phillip, 114
Callendar, Earl of, 151
Cambridge, 19, 95
Camby, Captain, 142-143
Carew, Major, 33, 37
Carlisle, 157
Carnaby, Colonel Francis, 78, 129, 133
Cavendish, Sir Charles, 137
Cavendish, William, Earl of Newcastle, 6-8, 10-12, 18-21, 25, 28-30, 36, 44-47, 49, 53-53,

61, 63-66, 68, 71, 74-75, 77, 79, 82-84, 86, 92-93, 96-99, 106, 109-114, 117, 120-125, 127, 129-130, 136-137, 140, 142, 144-149, 151, 157, 159
Cawood, 28, 87-89, 103, 121, 139, 144
Charles I, 7, 11, 14-20, 25, 36, 47-47, 53, 63, 82, 93, 95, 97, 100-101, 116, 120, 146-148, 151, 153-154, 157, 159
Charles II, 17, 19, 101, 157
Chester, 148, 153
Cholmley, Sir Hugh, 18, 45-47, 131, 140, 146
Clarendon, Earl of, 37
Clavering, Sir Robert, 145, 148
Clifford, Henry, Earl of Cumberland, 18, 20
Clifton Moor, 48-49
Coalley Chapel, 33
Constable, Sir William, 98, 150
Copley, Captain (later Colonel), 73, 156-157
Corbridge, 97
Cork, Earl of, 36
Crawford, Colonel Laurence, 114-115, 125, 127-128, 132, 136, 138, 141-142
Crawford-Lindsay, Earl of, 107, 138-141
Crofton Chapel, 43
Cromwell, Oliver, 12, 61, 94-96, 123-125, 127, 130-133, 136, 139-144, 151, 153, 157, 159
Dacre, Sir Richard, 129
Daventry, 152
Denbigh, Earl of, 120
Denton, 17
Derby, Earl of, 116
Devereux, Robert, Earl of Essex, 7, 19, 36, 95, 100, 147
Digby, Lord George, 18, 154, 157
Doncaster, 18, 99, 151-152, 154
Douglas, Robert, 134, 137, 139-1
40, 150
Drogheda, 95,
Dudley, Sir Gamaliel, 152-153
Dunbar, 95
Durham, 98
Eddington, Colonel, 31
Edgehill, 13, 95, 100
Eglinton, Earl of, 126, 134
Evers, Colonel, 30
Evers, Lord, 30
Eyre, Colonel Rowland, 129
Fairfax, Lady, 84
Fairfax, Lord Ferdinando, 6, 9-13, 17-21, 23-31, 44-45, 47, 49, 54-56, 60-61, 63-67, 71, 73-74, 76, 79, 81, 87, 92-96, 98-99, 101-103, 105-107, 109, 111-113, 125-127, 136-137, 139, 144, 148, 150-153, 156-157
Fairfax, Major, 135
Fairfax, Lord Thomas, 11

Fairfax, Sir Thomas, 11-12, 16-17, 20-21, 24-27, 29, 36, 38-39, 43-44, 47-52, 55-61, 66-69, 71-79, 83-84, 86-87, 89, 92-96, 98-99, 101-107, 114, 116, 121-123, 125-126, 132-135, 137-139
Fairfax, Sir William, 39, 41, 56
Fenwick, Colonel John, 142
Ferrybridge, 29-30, 101, 154, 157
Forbes, Sergeant-Major-General, 39, 41, 43, 67
Foulis, Sir Henry, 39, 52, 56, 84
Fraser, Colonel, 139, 142
Frescheville, Colonel John, 129
Fuller, Thomas, 122, 136, 139-140
Gainsborough, 93
Gell, Sir John, 53
Gifford, Major-General, 27, 56-60, 67-68, 71, 75-77, 84
Glemham, Sir Thomas, 20, 96, 145, 147
Gloucester, 100
Goodrick, Sir John, 31, 33
Goring, Colonel George, 31, 35-37, 50-52, 57-58, 60, 118, 120, 122, 129, 132-135, 141, 143-144, 147
Grandison, Lord, 130
Great Houghton, 6
Hague, The, 100
Hale Ford, 118
Halifax, 8, 18, 30-31, 43, 47, 55, 67, 77, 79, 87, 92-93, 99
Hamburg, 147
Hampden, John, 15
Harley, 53
Hartlepool, 98
Haselrigg, Sir Arthur, 15
Hastings, 49
Haughton, Captain, 129-130
Haughton, Sir Gilbert, 129
Heath Hall, 60
Helmsley Castle, 151-152
Henrietta Maria, Queen, 14, 16, 18, 36, 45-47, 53, 61, 63-64, 100
Herne, Colonel, 73-78
Hessay, 116, 120, 126, 150-151
Heworth Moor, 16
Hilliard, Captain, 31
Hodgson, Captain John, 33-34, 43, 49-50, 52, 98
Holland, Earl of, 19
Holles, Denzil, 15
Hopton, Sir Ralph, 15
Hornby, 148
Horsfall, Lieutenant, 43
Hotham, Captain John, 15, 18, 20-21, 28, 47, 66, 79
Hotham, Sir John, 15-16, 18, 47, 66, 78, 81, 94, 154
Howard, Colonel, 72, 78
Howard, Sir Francis, 31
Howley Hall, 55, 64-66
Huddersfield, 44
Hull, 15-19, 46-47, 61, 66, 79, 84, 86-87, 89, 91-94, 96, 98, 105, 144, 154

Humby, Lord, 150
Hunslet, 39, 41, 99
Huntingdon, 95
Ingleton, 151
James I, King, 11
Jeffrey, Thomas, 50 52
Johnston, Dr Nathaniel, 60
Kidhall, 52
Killinghall Wood, 52
King, James, Lord Eythin, 12, 19, 45, 76, 97, 124-125, 130, 145-147
King's Manor, 106, 113-114
King's Manor Walk, 180
Kirby Lonsdale, 148
Kirton, Sir Posthumous, 75-77
Knaresborough, 116, 120, 151-152
Knutsford, 117
Lambert, John, 98-99, 126, 133-135, 150, 157
Lampton, Colonel, 59
Langdale, Sir Marmaduke, 97, 129, 152-154, 157
Latham, Mister, 33
Lathom House, 116-118
Leeds, 6, 8, 13, 17, 29-31, 37-39, 44-45, 47-49, 52-55, 63, 67, 79, 83-84, 86-87, 92, 99, 139, 151
Leeds Walk, 164
Lentall, William, 54, 61, 93
Leslie, Alexander, Earl of Leven, 96-98, 107, 112-113, 123, 127, 131-132, 134, 137, 139, 144, 148, 150
Leslie, David, 123, 127, 132, 139-142, 157
Levenson, Colonel Thomas, 127
Lilburne, John, 127, 139, 142, 156
Lilly, William, 142
Lincoln, 93, 107
Lister, Captain William, 27-28
Lister, Joseph, 72, 82-84
Liverpool, 100, 119-120
London, 11, 16-16, 100
Long Marston, 123, 125-126, 132
Lucas, Margaret, Duchess of Newcastle, 19-21, 24-25, 28, 45-46, 50, 52-54, 64, 68, 72, 74-78, 92, 131, 140, 142, 146
Lucas, Sir Charles, 19, 129, 133, 135, 138-141, 144
Lucas, Sir Gervase, 99
Ludlow, Edmund, 131
Lumsden, Sir James, 111, 113, 138-139
Lyell, Colonel, 139
Maison, Captain, 78
Mallory, Sir John, 151, 157
Markham, Sir Clement, 16
Malton, 46, 99
Manchester, 47, 107, 118-119, 121
Manchester, Earl of, 94, 107-108, 110-111, 113-115, 127, 129-130, 133, 136, 138-139, 144, 151
Marston Moor, 6, 9, 11, 13, 17, 19, 36, 59, 95, 101, 120-122,129, 131-132, 144-145, 149, 157, 159
Marston Moor Walk, 185
Maurice, Prince, 100
Mayney, Sir John, 151
Mazine, Captain, 137
Meldrum, Sir John, 18, 94, 98-99, 102, 107, 119-121, 148, 152
Micklethwaite, Captain, 135
Mildmay, Captain, 39, 41, 43, 67, 71
Molyneux, Lord, 127, 140

Monkton, Sir Philip, 134, 154
Montague, Colonel, 150
Montrose, Marquis of, 154, 157
Moone, Joshua, 104-105
Moore, Colonel, 120
Morpeth, 96
Mud, Captain, 84
Musgrave, Sir Philip, 148
Nantwich, 17, 98, 116
Naseby, 9,13, 17, 95, 101, 153
Naylor, James, 41
Needham, Colonel, 102
Newark, 56, 64, 98-100, 102, 111, 151-153, 157
Newburn, 15
Newbury, 95, 100
Newcastle-upon-Tyne, 15, 25, 45, 96-97, 151
Newmarket, 47
Newport, Earl of, 18, 21, 25, 28, 31, 35, 45, 86
Norwich, Earl of, 36
Nottingham, 14, 18, 100
Oakwell Hall, 77
Ogden, Mister, 148
Oxford, 82, 159
Philiphaugh, 157
Pickering, 98
Piercebridge, 20
Pitscottie, Lieutenant-Colonel, 138
Pocklington, 46
Pontefract, 29, 44, 63-64, 103, 111, 113, 151-153, 157
Portsmouth, 36
Porter, Colonel George, 99, 129, 138, 144
Powick Bridge, 13, 100
Prague, 100
Preston, 120
Pym, John, 15
Quarrington Hill, 98
Ramsden, Sir John, 105
Reading, 100
Richmond, 148
Rigby, Colonel, 118
Rotherham, 8, 54, 157
Rowton Heath, 154
Rupert, Prince, 20, 36, 99-101, 107-108, 111-113, 115-125, 128-132, 136, 140-142, 145-149, 151, 157, 159
Rushworth, John, 118
Sabden Brook, 117
Sandal Castle, 151-153
Saville, Sir John, 64, 152
Saville, Sir William, 30, 39, 43, 54, 96
Scarborough, 18, 45-47, 141, 147, 151-153
Schofield, Mister, 43
Scott, Major, 137
Seacroft, 50, 52
Seacroft Moor, 8-9, 13, 17, 35-36, 45, 50-54, 84, 98
Selby, 13, 17, 28-31, 44, 47, 59, 79, 87, 89, 92-93, 98-99, 101-102, 106-107, 139
Selby Walk, 176
Sheffield, 54, 151
Sherburn-in-Elmet, 23, 29, 47, 49, 154, 156-157
Skipton, 11, 120, 151-153, 157
Slingsby, Sir Charles, 142
Slingsby, Sir Henry, 24-26, 28,

63, 66, 69, 73, 113-114, 129-130, 140, 142, 145, 149-151
Somerville, James, 141-142
South Milford, 157
Stamford Bridge, 49, 93, 99
Stanley, 56
Stewart, Captain William, 123, 132, 134, 136, 138-140
Stockdale, Thomas, 67, 69, 79, 93, 121, 123, 137
Stockport, 118
Strickland, Sir Thomas, 105
Strode, William, 15
Sunderland, 97-98
Tadcaster, 13, 20-21, 23-24, 29, 45, 48-49, 98, 102, 106, 121, 123
Tadcaster Walk, 160
Talbot, Captain, 77
Tankersley, 6, 53
Thirsk, 148
Thorner, 52
Thorpe Arch, 49
Throckmorton, Colonel, 78
Tickhill Castle, 151
Tillier, Colonel Henry, 120, 129
Tockwith, 124-126
Towton, 49
Trevor, Colonel Marcus, 127, 136
Tuke, Colonel Samuel, 128-129
Turnham Green, 100
Tyldesley, Sir Thomas, 127
Tynemouth, 100
Urry, Sir John, 127, 131
Vane, Sir Henry, 113
Van Tromp, Admiral, 47
Vaughan, Sir William, 127
Vere, Lord, 36
Vermuyden, Colonel Bartholomew, 127
Vlotho, 100, 125
Wakefield, 6, 13, 17, 30-31, 36, 38-39, 44-45, 52-56, 61, 63-64, 66-67, 71, 86, 92, 118, 122, 151
Wakefield Walk, 168
Waller, Sir William, 15
Walton, Captain Valentine, 130-131
Warrington, 118
Warwick, Sir Philip, 74
Watson, Leonard, 129, 132, 136, 104, 142, 144
Welbeck, 19, 96, 151
Wentbridge, 152
Wetherby, 20-21, 23, 116, 120
Wexford, 95
Whitehall, 157, 159
Widdrington, Sir Edward, 129
Wigan, 120
Williams, Captain, 104
Wilson, Captain, 44
Wilstrop Wood, 126, 140
Winceby, 95-96
Windsor, 16
Winn Moor, 50
Worcester, 96
Worksop, 154
Wortley, Sir Francis, 53
Wren, Colonel, 157
Yarm Bridge, 45-47
York, 11, 16-18, 20-21, 23, 44-47, 49, 61, 63, 84, 92-93, 96-100, 103-104, 106-109, 112-113, 116-117, 120-122, 125-126, 132, 134, 138, 140-149, 151, 159
York, Duke of, 16